A Short Introduction to
Helping Young People Manage Anxiety

JKP SHORT INTRODUCTIONS SERIES

JKP Short Introductions are the perfect starting point for any parent or professional who is caring for children or young people. Covering a range of key issues relating to mental health and well-being, these clear and easy to read books are packed with practical advice, tips and real-life examples. They are ideal for anyone working to help children to overcome problems and to develop healthy, happy and confident lives.

other books in the series

A Short Introduction to Understanding and Supporting Children and Young People Who Self-Harm
Carol Fitzpatrick
ISBN 978 1 84905 281 8
eISBN 978 0 85700 584 7

A Short Introduction to Promoting Resilience in Children
Colby Pearce
ISBN 978 1 84905 118 7
eISBN 978 0 85700 231 0

A Short Introduction to Attachment and Attachment Disorder
Colby Pearce
ISBN 978 1 84310 957 0
eISBN 978 1 84642 949 1

of related interest

Starving the Anxiety Gremlin
A Cognitive Behavioural Therapy Workbook on Anxiety Management for Young People
Kate Collins-Donnelly
ISBN 978 1 84905 341 9
eISBN 978 0 85700 673 8

Can I tell you about Anxiety?
A guide for friends, family and professionals
Lucy Willetts and Polly Waite
Illustrated by Kaiyee Tay
Part of the Can I tell you about...? series
ISBN 978 1 84905 527 7
eISBN 978 1 84905 527 7

Carol Fitzpatrick

A Short Introduction to
Helping Young People
People
Manage
Anxiety

Jessica Kingsley *Publishers*
London and Philadelphia

First published in 2015
by Jessica Kingsley Publishers
73 Collier Street
London N1 9BE, UK
and
400 Market Street, Suite 400
Philadelphia, PA 19106, USA

www.jkp.com

Library of Congress Cataloging in Publication Data
Fitzpatrick, Carol.
A short introduction to helping young people manage anxiety / Carol Fitzpatrick.
pages cm
Includes bibliographical references and index.
ISBN 978-1-84905-557-4 (alk. paper)
1. Anxiety in adolescence. 2. Anxiety disorders--Treatment. I. Title.
RJ506.A58F58 2015
616.85'2200835--dc23
2014030707

British Library Cataloguing in Publication Data
A CIP catalogue record for this book is available from the British Library

ISBN 978 1 84905 557 4
eISBN 978 0 85700 989 0

Printed and bound in Great Britain

CONTENTS

PREFACE

This book was written in response to requests from parents and teachers about how best to help young people with anxiety. Problematic anxiety is very common in young people and can vary from mild fears that are just a nuisance, at one end of the spectrum, to severely incapacitating disorders that impact greatly on both the young person and their family, at the other end. Being a parent, carer or teacher of a young person with problematic anxiety can be a daunting experience. Anxiety often feels 'contagious', and when dealing with an anxious young person it is not uncommon to feel one's own anxiety, frustration and anger levels rising and to feel powerless to help. But having a supportive adult is a huge asset for the young person, and there is much you can do to help.

The book has a positive, down-to-earth approach in dealing with the day-to-day problems that coping with anxiety can bring. It has good ideas about how parents and carers can help by how they respond to and support anxious young people and how they can encourage them to use researched self-help approaches that have been shown to work. The case reports are based on real-life situations, with names and details changed to ensure confidentiality.

I have written the book based on more than 30 years' experience as a child psychiatrist, during which I have learned so much from the young people and families I have worked with. I would like to thank them for the richness of that experience. I would also like to thank my colleagues in the Mater Child and Adolescent Mental Health Service and in the Children's University Hospital, Temple Street, Dublin, for their insights and encouragement over many years. Thank you also to my good friend, Deirdre Corrigan, who is a teacher who gave me much useful information and advice.

I am particularly grateful to my grown-up family for their inspiration and never failing encouragement. My husband John died suddenly when I was writing this book. His support was a source of great strength for me, and I dedicate this book to him.

CHAPTER 1

WHAT IS ANXIETY?

This chapter provides an introduction to and outline of the whole book. It explains the normal function of anxiety in everyday life and how anxiety shows itself in different ways at different stages of development. It explains problematic anxiety using the faulty thermostat metaphor. It explains how anxiety is the most common mental health difficulty and how it can be overt and apparent or hidden and how it often underlies negative, oppositional behaviour in young people. It acknowledges for readers how dealing with a young person who is suffering from significant anxiety can be difficult and frustrating, while emphasizing the importance of their support in helping young people to manage their anxiety.

KATY'S STORY

Katy is seven and loves dressing up and parties. She gets very excited when she is invited to a classmate's birthday party and spends ages planning what to wear, what present to bring and what she will eat. But she has never actually made it to a birthday party! When the day of the party arrives, she is usually very quiet and pale that morning, eats very little, is reluctant to get into her party clothes and tells her mum she does not want to go. Sometimes she can be persuaded to get into the car, but getting her out at the other end would be impossible without heartbreaking crying and a struggle that her parents are not prepared to engage in. Her parents feel very sorry for her, as they know how much she would like to go, but they also feel frustrated and angry, which they try to hide. This has happened many times, and now they feel like refusing any party invitations that come along, but Katy begs them not to, saying this time she will go. But she doesn't.

JOHN'S STORY

John is 14, and his life is not happy. He hates school, where he struggles with the work and has few friends. He often misses days because of minor ailments. He has different interests to many of the other boys and dislikes sport. Each morning he gets stomach cramps as he anticipates the day ahead and worries that he may be called upon to speak in front of the class. He goes out of his way to avoid being 'picked on' by teachers or peers. Mondays are worst, with five whole days of school ahead. He is happiest when at home in his room listening to music, which helps him to forget about his worries.

John has always been a worrier, and school has never been easy for him. He just about managed in primary school, but he has found secondary school much more difficult, both academically and socially. His parents split up a year ago, which affected him a lot. He worries a great deal that his dad, who he sees regularly, might get beaten up when he is on the night shift in his taxi. His mum's financial problems are another source of worry. His siblings don't seem to have the same worries and tell him: 'Get a life.'

Anxiety is something everyone is familiar with. It is part of the range of normal human emotions, such as happiness, sadness, excitement or disappointment, and it plays an important part in survival. The feeling of anxiety is associated with a heightened level of arousal in the brain and increased activity in the nerves that supply the heart and muscles, preparing the person for 'flight or fight' in situations of threat. This is all good when there is real threat and you need to be able to flee or fight, such as when you see a car approaching as you are crossing the road or hear your smoke alarm going off during the night. It is less than useful when anxiety is provoked by everyday events, such as having a conversation with someone, eating in public, going into a shop or by nothing in particular. It is as if the anxiety control mechanism in the brain is not working properly, and an anxiety response is being switched on when there is no need. It is similar to a faulty thermostat in a central heating system. The thermostat is supposed to switch the system on when the temperature falls below a certain level and switch it off when the temperature goes above that level. If it is faulty, it may switch the system on at a different temperature or even cause the system to be on all the time. Young people with anxiety problems have anxiety 'thermostats' that are over-sensitive and faulty – they switch on anxiety responses that are 'out of sync' with the reality of the threat presented or remain on all the time. Chapter 2 will discuss what is known about why some people are more prone to this than others.

As well as unpleasant feelings, anxiety can affect people in many other ways, including:

- thought processes:
  - » difficulty with concentration
  - » difficulty making decisions
  - » 'startling' easily
  - » becoming confused
  - » going blank
  - » irritability

- breathing:
  - » hyperventilating
  - » sensation of being unable to breathe deeply enough

- heart:
  - » rapid heart rate
  - » palpitations

- digestive system:
  - » nausea
  - » abdominal cramps
  - » sensation of needing to pass a bowel motion but being unable to
  - » frequent bowel motions

- urinary system:
  - » need to pass urine at frequent intervals
  - » bed-wetting.

It may be very obvious that a young person is suffering from anxiety. Young children often seek repeated reassurance from parents, although the reassurance seems to have little effect in the long term. Older children and teenagers may keep their thoughts to themselves, and their anxiety may only show itself in their behaviour. For example, they may avoid situations that make them anxious, such as attending a family gathering or going to school, or just seem to be distracted and irritable. They often think they are 'going mad', which is one of the reasons they find it hard to talk about what they are experiencing. It can be much harder to recognize that problematic anxiety underlies the difficulties of such a young person.

ANXIETY DISORDERS

While anxiety is a normal emotion, when it is experienced to a severe degree and is interfering with the young person's ability to get on with life, it is defined as an anxiety disorder. Anxiety disorders are the most common mental health problems in children and teenagers. Research has shown that about 3 per cent of young people suffer from anxiety disorders and that relatively few of them are referred for treatment (Meltzer *et al.* 2000). This is a pity, as anxiety disorders respond well to treatment, which does not necessarily have to be drawn out and intensive. For more information, see Chapter 7, which deals with getting professional help.

Anxiety disorders are categorized as if they were separate and easily distinguishable conditions, but in reality they often overlap and have many features in common.

Generalized anxiety disorder (GAD)

This is where the anxiety is generalized and persistent – the chronically anxious young person who worries a great deal, is apprehensive when dealing with anything new and who may have a variety of physical symptoms of anxiety, such as difficulty with breathing or panic attacks, which come to the fore at particularly stressful times.

Phobias

This is where the anxiety symptoms are extreme and are focused only on a particular object, such as a spider, or event, such as passing urine in school. The person often takes extreme steps to avoid phobic situations. *Agoraphobia* refers to a number of related phobias that tend to occur together. These include fear of leaving home alone, fear of being in an enclosed space and fear of being anywhere from which there is not an easily accessible exit or where help may not be immediately available should one collapse or fall ill. These symptoms may result in the young person becoming housebound or only being able to be out and about when accompanied.

Separation anxiety disorder

Separation anxiety is a normal part of development in babies and toddlers, where it shows itself as fear of strangers, clinging to familiar figures and crying when separated from them. The key feature is anxiety that is prevented by the presence of a familiar figure. When this happens in older children and teenagers, and is interfering significantly in their lives, it is called a separation anxiety disorder. Features may include extreme upset on separation from familiar figures, constant worry about possible harm coming to close family members, being unable to sleep alone or being unable to attend school.

Social anxiety disorder

This disorder is present when anxiety symptoms occur mainly in social situations and lead to marked avoidance of such situations. Many children and teenagers are 'shy' and dislike social situations, such as being focused on in public, but in social anxiety disorder the person's life is affected negatively by their extreme discomfort and avoidance of social situations. Often the anxiety shows itself with physical symptoms, such as trembling, palpitations, sweating, blushing and dizziness, as well as a strong wish to escape from the situation. These difficulties may lead the young person to miss out on a whole range of experiences and to become lonely and isolated.

Panic disorder

Panic attacks vary from person to person, but have a number of features in common. They come on suddenly, are often unpredictable and are accompanied by physical symptoms such as palpitations, a sensation of being unable to breathe deeply enough, dizziness and, most distressingly, feelings of impending death or loss of control. They are so frightening that they lead people to avoid situations where they think they may have a panic attack. While isolated, 'low-grade' panic attacks are not uncommon in the general population, a 'panic disorder' is the term used when panic attacks impact on people's lives to a level where they are not able to function normally.

Obsessive compulsive disorder (OCD)

It used to be thought that obsessive compulsive disorders were rare, but as more studies looked at psychological symptoms in the general population, and people have become more open about talking about such symptoms, we now know that obsessive compulsive symptoms are relatively common. It is only when they are severe and interfering with the person's ability to lead a normal life that they are referred to as obsessive compulsive disorder or OCD. In this disorder the person is troubled by repetitive thoughts, images or impulses, accompanied by compulsive rituals or routines that they feel they have to do in order to reduce the anxiety associated with the obsessions. OCD has its onset in childhood or early adolescence in most cases and can be extremely distressing, as most young people do not tell anyone about their experiences and often believe they are 'going mad'. It usually only comes to adult attention when a parent observes some of the unusual behaviour and is able to talk to the young person about it. Please see Chapter 6 for further information.

Selective mutism

This is much less common than the other anxiety disorders but is one of the most intriguing. It is characterized by a persistent failure to speak in certain social situations where speaking is expected, while speaking in other situations. In recent years it has been categorized as an anxiety disorder, with an understanding that it is extreme anxiety that prevents the child from speaking. The child typically does not speak in school, while speaking with ease within the family. Please see Chapter 6 for further information.

WHAT ABOUT 'HIDDEN' ANXIETY?

Most of us can empathize with a young person suffering from anxiety, particularly if there are visible signs of anxiety present. It is relatively easy to 'put oneself in the shoes' of someone who is pale, quiet, trembling or hyperventilating. But it is not so easy to empathize when the young person's symptoms are less clear-cut. The child with abdominal pain, who only gets the pain on school mornings and whose pain seems to clear up if they are allowed to stay home or come home, can be most frustrating for parents and teachers, and suspicion can arise that they are 'putting it on'. The behaviour of the young person who is negative and oppositional, but who is inwardly dealing with marked anxiety but is unable to talk about it, can understandably lead to rows and conflict, which make the situation worse all round. A great deal of patience is needed to prevent getting into a 'downward spiral' of conflict with such young people. Some of the ideas in this book may be helpful in preventing this from happening.

JACK'S STORY

Jack has many obsessions about which he is deeply ashamed. He worries that if he does not follow a particular routine in the mornings and evenings then something terrible will happen to his parents. The routine is taking longer and longer as time goes by, as he has to repeat each step numerous times until it feels that he has got it 'right'. His morning routine involves repeated washing of his hands (in case he spreads infection), putting on his clothes in a certain order, making his bed in a particular way so that each fold is symmetrical and checking that his bedroom window is locked before he leaves the room. He has to get up earlier and earlier to get through all this and still be on time for school, but despite his best efforts he is often late for his lift with his dad, which causes daily rows.

Jack has not told anyone about his 'routines'. He thinks he may be 'going mad', as at one level he knows his fears are senseless, but he can't stop them. He is very irritable both at home and at school, and people are starting to avoid him. His mum knows something is wrong, but he just snaps at her when she asks him if he is okay.

ANXIETY AND THE FAMILY

A young person's anxiety problems can have a ripple effect on the whole family. Often parents feel their own anxiety becoming problematic as they struggle to help their child. Sometimes parents have very different and even opposing views of how best to manage the child with anxiety, leading to conflict between themselves. Siblings usually do not understand the child's difficulties and are often angry at the extra attention given to the child with anxiety. The impact of being late for school or work or missing an outing because of the anxious child's behaviour affects everyone and can lead to much family conflict. In addition, parents often have to cope with conflicting advice from members of the extended family. Most parents will be familiar with, 'There's nothing wrong with that child' or, 'She's not like that when she's with me' and so forth. Such advice, while meant to be helpful, is enough to engender feelings of rage in the calmest parent!

While most research has focused on family stress, many studies have shown that family support can make a world of difference to the anxious child. Families can provide understanding, tolerance and hope, as well as that fine balance between accepting the child's difficulties while encouraging them to manage and overcome them.

My mum helped me a lot through that year. I sometimes lashed out at her, but she was always there for me.

(Linda, aged 15, talking about how she coped with anxiety and depression when she moved from primary to secondary school.)

CHAPTER 2

WHY ARE SOME YOUNG PEOPLE MORE ANXIOUS THAN OTHERS?

Recent research in the area of neuroscience has helped us to start making sense of how the complex interplay of genetic factors, personality factors (many of which are genetically determined), and life experience can lead to problematic anxiety. There is much we still do not understand about why some people are more anxious than others, but research in this area is moving forward all the time.

THE BROWN FAMILY

The Browns are a caring family. Jane, the mother, struggles to cope with her many roles – supportive wife, caring mother, competent work colleague and good friend. She rarely relaxes, almost always feels stressed and does not think she is particularly good at any of her roles. Don, the father, is a relaxed, easy-going person, who enjoys his work, is involved with the children and has a good work–life balance. He is supportive to Jane and tries to help with all she has to cope with, but as he rarely does these things as well as she does, this often leads to conflict between them.

Their son, Tom, is five. He is a cautious, anxious child, who is a very fussy eater. He worries about running out of petrol or crashing when in the car, about the dark and monsters at night and about eating his lunch in school, where the expectation is that everything will be eaten. When his parents have a row, he repeatedly says he is sorry, although the row often has nothing to do with him, and he repeatedly tells his parents that he loves them. He does not seem to enjoy life very much.

Chloe, their daughter, is three. She is a happy-go-lucky child, who is outgoing and enthusiastic and will eat almost anything. She settled easily in crèche and seems to enjoy going there. She rarely cries, except when she falls over or is very tired. When her parents have a row, she does not seem to notice and continues playing. Don and Jane often marvel at how different two children can be.

Continued on page 23.

One of the most fascinating aspects of families is how different family members can be. As with most of our characteristics and behaviours, a tendency towards anxiety is shaped by a complex interplay of genetic factors, personality factors and our life experiences. These different factors interact with one another throughout our lives in a way that we are only beginning to understand.

GENETIC FACTORS

Research into the genetics of anxiety has made great strides in recent years, but, as with most genetic studies, the more we find out, the more complex the picture becomes! There is no single gene for anxiety, but what seems to be passed from parent to child are a number of single genes that act together to confer a vulnerability to develop anxiety.

Whether or not the child actually develops anxiety is dependent on aspects of their personality and their life experiences. Genes probably produce their effects through the role they play in the manufacture and behaviour of neurotransmitters, the minute chemicals in the brain that regulate the passage of electrical impulses from one brain cell to the next.

TEMPERAMENT AND PERSONALITY FACTORS

Studies have shown that some babies seem from the very earliest days to have an 'easy' temperament. They are soothed by being held; they have regular sleep and waking cycles; they feed well and with enjoyment. Other babies seem to be at the opposite end of the spectrum. They are difficult to feed and soothe; they startle easily, cry a lot and don't seem to enjoy being held. This pattern has been labelled a 'difficult' temperamental style. Temperamental style is not set in stone, and often changes as the baby becomes older, but, despite this, children who have had 'difficult' temperaments as babies have higher rates of anxiety and behaviour problems in childhood than those who have had 'easy' temperaments.

As most parents know, it is much easier to be a 'good enough' parent to a baby who has an 'easy' temperament. Such babies elicit positive and calm responses from others, leading those who care for them to feel positive, calm and competent. Thus, a positive cycle is set up, whereby the behaviour of the baby and their care giver influence each other in a cyclical way, leading each to feel good about themselves and making the cycle continue. Current research suggests that when babies have their needs met in a predictable and positive way, the pathways in their brains that lead to soothing of unpleasant emotional states are stimulated and develop, leading in time to the ability of the child to 'self-soothe'. This may help to explain why babies with 'easy' temperaments have lower levels of anxiety and behaviour problems in childhood than those who have had 'difficult' temperaments.

People with any type of personality can develop anxiety disorders, but people with certain personality types are more at risk than others. Young people who are shy and introverted with low levels of self-confidence are more likely to develop anxiety disorders, but this raises the question of whether low levels of anxiety caused the shyness and introversion in the first place. The same question could be asked in relation to the increased rates of anxiety disorders in people who are perfectionists: which came first – the anxiety or the perfectionism?

LIFE EXPERIENCES

During my child psychiatry training many years ago, I was taught that we are born with brains that are 'hard wired' with various nerve tracts and pathways that grow and become more active as we develop, but that few other changes happen over time. We now know that this is not accurate. Research in recent years has shown that the way in which nerve tracts and pathways in the brain develop is very much influenced by our life experience, which actually shapes how the brain grows and develops.

Early life stress

Research has shown that children who have experienced early life stress are at increased risk of developing anxiety and behavioural problems in later childhood. Early life stress may take many forms. It may be prenatal stress, where maternal stress leads to high levels of cortisol (the stress hormone) circulating in the mother and having an effect on the development and functioning of the foetus's brain pathways, which control reactions to stress.

Other forms of early life stress include maternal separation and child neglect or abuse. Children exposed to such experiences are at increased risk of developing anxiety and other disorders, and current research shows that such stress also acts by affecting the development and functioning of the child's brain pathways (Lupien *et al.* 2009). Not all children exposed to early life stress go on to develop problems, which raises intriguing questions about what protects them and makes them resilient to stress.

THE BROWN FAMILY

Continued from page 20.

Jane's pregnancy with Tom was not straightforward. There was some bleeding in the early weeks, which led Jane to be anxious throughout the pregnancy. Labour was drawn out and not the experience Jane had hoped for. She was exhausted following the birth and for many weeks afterwards. She was determined to breastfeed, and did so for two weeks, but it was a 'nightmare', as Tom never seemed to get enough. Her mother and Don begged her to give it up, as she was unable to eat or sleep herself at that stage.

Tom was not an easy baby. He cried a lot and was difficult to comfort. The evenings were particularly bad, and Don spent many hours driving around with Tom asleep in his baby seat, as this was the only way to get him to stop crying. Jane feared she was developing postnatal depression, as she often felt at the end of her tether, but these feelings improved when Tom was about three months old and became more settled. It was never as bad again, but those months were some of the hardest in Jane's life, and she vowed never to have another baby. But those memories faded, and when Tom was just two she became pregnant with Chloe.

The pregnancy with Chloe was very different. Although Jane was initially anxious about being pregnant, this eased off as the months went by and all seemed to be proceeding smoothly. Chloe's birth was straightforward, and she was an easy, contented baby who settled quite quickly into a routine that suited Jane. Tom became a bit clingy and demanding in the early months after Chloe's arrival, but his parents had been expecting that and were able to give him a bit of extra attention. He seemed to accept Chloe's arrival, and was often affectionate towards her.

Continued on page 26.

Stress in childhood

Childhood is often idealized as a time of excitement, happiness and contentment. Of course, it is like that some of the time. But stress is also a part of childhood, and many children live with high levels of stress. Bullying, being unable to cope academically and/or socially in school, high levels of anxiety and/or conflict at home, harsh and/or neglectful parenting, domestic violence, rejection by peers and violence in their communities – these are realities for many children. Such children are more prone to developing anxiety and other emotional and behavioural disorders, although not all do so. As with other forms of adversity, some children are more resilient than others.

RESILIENCE

There is no single factor that makes some children more resilient than others. Resilience is also the result of a complex interplay of genetic factors, personality and life experiences. Researchers at the University of California,

Los Angeles (UCLA) have recently discovered the oxytocin receptor (OXTR) gene, which is linked to psychological characteristics such as optimism and self-esteem (Saphire-Bernstein *et al.* 2011). As with other genetic studies, the researchers do not claim that this gene causes one to be optimistic but, rather, that some variations of the gene confer a vulnerability to be less optimistic.

Other factors known to be associated with resilience to adversity in children include the following:

- The child's IQ: While some very intelligent children are deeply troubled by anxiety, there is some evidence to suggest that, in general, children with higher IQs are more resilient to anxiety, probably because they are better at problem-solving and find it easier to make sense of their experience.

- The child's ability to regulate their emotional responses: Children with this ability are more likely to feel in control of themselves and their environment.

- Having a close supportive relationship with a parent or parent figure: Such a relationship makes children feel secure and loved, which in turn leads to them feeling loveable and raises their self-esteem.

- Being raised in a family where parenting style is warm and nurturing, with consistent discipline, structure and supervision.

- Being 'connected' in a positive way with peers, teachers and schools, and being involved in activities.

Parents can do a lot to increase resilience in young people by parenting them in a way that provides security, warmth and consistent relationships. People who care for children can help to increase their resilience by focusing on supporting them to learn how to regulate their emotional responses, develop social skills and improve their social connectedness.

THE BROWN FAMILY

Continued from page 24.
When Tom was five he started to wet the bed, having previously been dry at night. This happened shortly after he had started in 'big school' and Jane had started a new job.

Jane and Don wondered if he had developed a urinary tract infection, but the family doctor checked his urine and said it was normal. They took some time to discuss Tom and wondered what could be causing him stress. They realized that tension levels at home had been high in recent months. Both parents were feeling the stress resulting from Jane's new and more demanding job situation, and they resolved to do something to improve things. They supported each other in doing as many of the household jobs as possible in the evenings, which meant that mornings were not so chaotic, and Jane did not have to face cooking when she arrived home from work, having picked up the children from the crèche. They also resolved to get a babysitter and have a night out together at least once a month.

They took a calm and practical approach to Tom's bed-wetting. He got very upset when he wet the bed, but they explained that it was a common problem and was just a nuisance that would probably stop soon. They bought a waterproof mattress cover and offered Tom the option of wearing 'pull-up' pants at night, which he sometimes chose to do. This cut down on washing bedclothes.

They had a chat with Tom's teacher, who reassured them that, although he was very quiet and self-contained for the first few weeks in school, he now seemed more relaxed and was making friends with some of the children in his class. This information helped them to feel more relaxed about Tom.

The bed-wetting gradually stopped after a few months, and Tom seemed happier and more confident. He remained a cautious, rather serious child, but was not as anxious, and this helped his parents to be more relaxed about him.

While parents can do nothing to change their child's genetic vulnerability, nor to shape their earliest temperamental characteristics, they can do much to promote their resilience by a warm, nurturing and consistent parenting style, fostering their social behaviour and relationships and by dealing calmly and effectively with the inevitable ups and downs of life that their children experience.

CHAPTER **3**

APPROACHES THAT WORK WITH ANXIOUS YOUNG PEOPLE

This chapter addresses the contagious effect of anxiety and the frustration often felt by those who care for young people with problematic anxiety. It emphasizes the importance of a calm approach and gives ideas about how this can be achieved. Communication strategies are discussed, as this can be an area of particular difficulty with anxious young people. Problem-solving and rehearsal are described. It looks at the role of routine, diet and exercise. The importance of self-care for the adults involved is highlighted.

Being with an anxious person can make one very anxious. We don't fully understand how this occurs. It can happen to parents, teachers, relatives or friends. It is as if the anxious young person gives off an 'aura' that is picked up by those around them. Those with a very close relationship to the young person do not even have to be with them to 'feel' their anxiety. And it does not stop there! The anxious young person can sense the anxiety of the caregiver, making their own anxiety worse, and a vicious cycle is set up. Add to that the frustration and anger generated by an anxious young person's refusal to do as we ask, and the guilt often felt by parents who feel their child's anxiety is somehow due to their parenting, and it is not difficult to understand how things can get out of hand.

MANAGING YOUR OWN ANXIETY

It is much easier to change your own behaviour than to change anyone else's. But when you change how you react in situations with anxious young people, you may find that the young person's reaction changes also.

Pressing the pause button

This technique is useful in any situation where you find your own anxiety, frustration or anger rising. It involves pausing, taking a deep breath, counting slowly to yourself and taking a mental step back from a difficult situation. This gives you time to chose how to respond and allows you to be in control of your own reactions. It may mean calmly walking away from the situation to allow yourself to calm down and decide how best to proceed. This avoids conflict escalating and things getting out of hand. With older children, it may be helpful to give a brief explanation such as, 'I need a bit of time to calm down.' You can then choose how and when to address the issue, ideally when both you and the young person are calmer.

MS SMYTH'S STORY

Ms Smyth, a drama teacher, had put a lot of work into helping Becky to prepare for her role in the school musical. Becky, aged 15, had severe social anxiety, mixed very poorly with her classmates and often missed school. She had initially refused to have anything to do with plans for the musical, but with encouragement and a great deal of support from Ms Smyth, she had agreed to take a small, non-speaking part and had attended rehearsals regularly.

On the first night of the show, Becky got into her costume, but five minutes before the curtain was due to go up, she told Ms Smyth that she could not do it and that she was not going to take part. Ms Smyth tried to encourage her, but Becky was adamant. Ms Smyth could feel her own anger rising. She remembered all the time she had given to Becky and thought of the disappointment of Becky's parents, who had been delighted when they learned that she would be taking part in the musical. She felt like saying something very hurtful to Becky, but instead she pressed the pause button, took a deep breath and told Becky she would discuss things with her after the show when they were both calmer.

The next day, Ms Smyth was calmer. She noticed that Becky was despondent, and when she spoke with her, she learned that Becky had very much wanted to do the show but had become paralysed with anxiety at the thought of all those people looking at her. Becky, who had previously refused all offers of help, agreed to allow Ms Smyth to talk with her mother about getting some help to deal with her social anxiety, which was holding her back in many areas of her life.

Planning to give yourself time

If you are prone to anxiety then having to be in a certain place at a certain time, such as work or school, is likely to make you flustered. This is made worse if the cause of your lateness is a child who can't or won't hurry up. Planning to give yourself time can reduce your stress.

Many families face a potentially explosive situation every school morning, when one (or more) of the children makes everyone late. It can be made somewhat less stressful by getting as many things as possible (uniform, school bag, lunches, sports gear) ready the night before. Younger children often welcome this routine but teenagers rarely do. It may be necessary to discuss the situation with your teenager when you are both calm and to agree a plan, which may involve you leaving them behind to make their own way to school or to face the consequences of not attending if they cannot be ready on time. This needs to be thought out carefully in advance, as it may not be the best approach if your teenager does not want to attend school in the first place.

Talking to someone

Being able to talk to someone about how you are feeling can be invaluable. It may be someone you trust, which may be your partner, a good friend or a work colleague. Often the very act of being able to put words to your feelings can help. Your GP may be a useful source of help or may recommend a counsellor who is experienced in helping people manage anxiety.

Looking after your own physical and mental health

There is a vast body of research showing the importance of a healthy lifestyle for both physical and mental health. Exercise is good for general health, and some but not all studies have shown it to be an effective treatment for anxiety (Larun *et al.* 2006). It is not certain how this works, but exercise is known to lead to the release of neurotransmitters and endorphins in the brain – chemicals that elevate mood and give a 'feel-good' factor. Exercise also helps to distract from negative thoughts, which are very common occurences when people are stressed.

Exercise conjures up ideas of running or doing workouts, which appeal to some people, but other forms of exercise can be just as effective. Dancing, walking and some forms of yoga are other types of exercise that can be done alone but also in groups, the latter providing the added benefit of a 'social connection' element, which has been shown to be another factor in maintaining positive mental health.

The benefits of a balanced diet are well known, as is the importance of avoiding cigarettes and excessive alcohol. This is easier said than done. Nicotine has an anxiety-relieving effect, but this only lasts for the short time it is in your system, and when it wears off the anxiety returns, leading to the need for another cigarette. A glass of wine in the evenings may be good for you, but if it is gradually turning into a half bottle and then a bottle, it is time to look for other ways of coping!

Meditation, yoga and practising mindfulness have all been shown to be effective in reducing anxiety. Many excellent courses are available, some of which are accessible online for free.

KEEPING CONNECTED

It is easy when coping with a young person with problematic anxiety to let your world become narrower and more and more focused on the young person. This is not good for either of you. Having your own interests and taking time for your other relationships helps you to recharge your batteries and return refreshed to the problematic situation. There is good evidence that being socially connected to others, whether it is with family, friends or as part of a community activity, is associated with good mental health (Shields and Wheatley Price 2005). Contact with others also helps to keep your own problems in perspective, as you will meet many others who are coping with difficulties.

By trying the above approaches, you are not only taking positive steps to manage your own anxiety, you are also modelling healthy ways of coping for the young person in your care.

STRATEGIES TO HELP THE YOUNG PERSON MANAGE THEIR ANXIETY

Externalizing the problem

Studies of 'what works in therapy' have shown that externalizing the problem can be useful (Thomas 2002). It helps the young person to view the anxiety, not as an integral part of themselves, but rather as an unwelcome intruder, over which they can gain some control. It gives the message to the young person that *they* are not the problem, rather that the problem (anxiety) is the problem.

With young children, this may involve giving the anxiety a name, which the child chooses, such as 'Mr Meany', and explaining that when Mr Meany is around he makes things seem very scary, even when they are not really scary. The idea is then conveyed to the child that there are things they can do to get Mr Meany to go away – for example, playing with a favourite toy, watching TV, playing a computer game or drawing or painting Mr Meany being pushed out. It is best to work on these ideas when the child is calm, so that when they are anxious they will be able to open their 'toolbox' of 'ways of getting rid of Mr Meany'. With young children, drawing, painting or Play-Doh can be used to help explain the concept.

With older children and teenagers, it is easier to explain the concept with words, although drawing and painting are also useful. You can explain that when anxiety takes over, it affects our brains and our bodies, leading to physical changes, such as a racing heart, difficulty breathing, sweating, and so on, and mental changes, such as worry, fear, dread, confusion, panic, and so forth. Ideas about what to do when this happens – how to 'boss' the anxiety away – should come from the teenagers themselves.

This approach helps to take some of the fear out of anxiety and to give the young person a sense of mastery and control.

'Worry time'

This is especially useful with young people who constantly seek reassurance or who wish to repeatedly discuss their worries. Parents explain to their child that there is going to be a time, usually in the evening, when one or the other parent will sit down with the child to discuss all the worries of the day. This will be their 'special time', without interruptions, and should generally last about 15 minutes. If the child wants to talk about their worries at other times or seeks repeated reassurance, then the parent calmly reminds them about 'worry time' and avoids getting into further conversation about worry issues at that time. Very persistent children (and they can be very persistent) who are concerned that they may have forgotten the particular issue by the time that it gets to their 'worry time' can be asked to write down or draw their worries to use as a reminder.

This approach may seem unkind, but it helps the child put a boundary on their anxiety and avoids the negative cycle that can so easily develop when an anxious child repeatedly seeks reassurance from an increasingly frustrated parent. Of course, it is important to stick to the plan and set aside the time in the evenings.

Keeping communication going

The opposite extreme to the anxious young person who constantly seeks reassurance is the one who never speaks about their feelings. Their caregivers can often recognize when their anxiety is particularly problematic – they may become pale, fidgety and increasingly silent or, less commonly, more talkative. Questions about how they are feeling at times like that are likely to get a curt response, such as, 'I'm fine', said with much anger, or maybe no response at all, which is very annoying! Rather than questioning them, it may work better to say nothing at the time, but later to comment, 'I notice you seemed a bit stressed today; is there any way I can help?' This is unlikely to lead to an 'opening up' at the time, but it does give the message that you are there for them and that you may be able to help. If they do choose to talk to you, 'active listening' seems to work better than giving reassurance or advice. This involves giving attention to what the young person is saying by not asking lots of questions and not coming up with possible solutions unless asked. Making brief comments ('that must have been upsetting') shows that you are interested and are trying to understand what the young person may be feeling. Our tendency as adults is to try to reassure, but this rarely has the desired effect and rather frustrates young people, who feel we don't really understand.

Rehearsal

Just as adults 'rehearse' for job interviews, many young people benefit from rehearsing how they will manage anxiety-provoking situations. For example, children who worry they will have no one to play with, or that other children 'won't be nice' to them, can be encouraged to practise a number of ways they could handle such situations. Using 'let's pretend', and keeping it light-hearted and fun, works best with young children, while teenagers often welcome a more serious approach.

Problem-solving

Problem-solving can be useful if the young person asks your advice or is seeking a solution. This involves setting aside time and 'actively listening' initially, and then asking the young person what, ideally, they would like to happen or what their goal would be. This leads to helping the young person to think about all the possible approaches to achieving that goal and selecting one approach to try. Sometimes progress is reviewed later and possibly another approach tried.

MARK'S STORY

Mark, aged ten, rarely left the house at weekends or during the school holidays. He spent most of his time at home playing computer games. He had been bullied in the past and was wary of other boys of his age. Mark heard that chess was played in a youth club in his area and wished he could go, but he told his dad he was too nervous. His dad set aside some time to 'problem-solve' with Mark. Mark was clear that he would love to go, so together they brainstormed a number of possible solutions. These included: going alone (too nervous), going with Dad who would stay with him (too embarrassing), asking one or two boys in his class who were interested in chess to see if they were going (too shy), and visiting the club with Dad before it started to meet the leader and get a feel for the place. They decided to try the last option, which worked well. Mark got on with the leader, who asked him to stay for a while that day, which he did. Having broken the ice, Mark felt comfortable attending the following week and became involved in the club.

The key to using these approaches successfully is to remain calm and 'matter of fact' about them. It may take trial and error to find an approach that appeals, but it is worth persisting, as many anxious young people find them useful.

CHAPTER **4**

HELPING ANXIOUS YOUNG PEOPLE MANAGE SCHOOL

School can be a daunting place for young people with problematic anxiety and can present considerable social and academic challenges. Providing support involves parents and teachers working together to try to understand the young person, and using approaches with which both are comfortable. This chapter describes useful strategies to help with school-related anxiety and discusses bullying in particular.

Anxiety can show itself in many different ways in the school setting. The quiet young person who keeps to themselves and takes steps to avoid being the focus of attention, the obsessively hard worker who takes hours longer than peers with homework, and the regular absentee who suffers from tummy pains or headaches on school days, but whose pains seem to disappear when they are allowed to stay home – these are all familiar presentations of anxiety. While many anxious young people are of average or above average intellectual ability, and should have no difficulty coping academically with school, their anxiety can interfere with their ability to learn, making school even more difficult for them. Young people who have a specific learning difficulty, such as with reading or maths, face considerable problems unless their learning difficulty is recognized and appropriate support given. Sometimes such young people mask their anxiety by behaving in a challenging, provocative manner, which may make it less likely that their learning difficulty will be recognized. It can be hard to determine which is the chicken and which is the egg in an anxious young person who is struggling academically, although an educational assessment carried out by a professional who is experienced in working with anxious young people may throw light on the subject.

Anxious young people often find relationships with peers particularly difficult. They may be perceived as 'different' by peers, making them more vulnerable to bullying and exclusion. On the other hand, they are often highly sensitive and perceive rejection when none is meant. The careful use of team tasks in the classroom, where each person has a part to play in getting the task done, can help an anxious young person gain confidence in dealing with peers.

COMMUNICATION BETWEEN PARENT AND TEACHER

Ideally, parent and teacher will be comfortable with each other and will discuss the young person's difficulties and approaches that they find helpful. This requires openness and trust, which is not always easy to achieve and may be impossible. Parents and teachers are human, and each may interpret any suggestion that the child has a problem as reflecting badly on their parenting or teaching skills. This can be overcome if both parent and teacher try to put themselves in the shoes of the other and see things from each other's viewpoint. In the first instance, a parent who has concerns about their child's school-related anxiety could approach the teacher, mentioning the concerns and asking the teacher how, in their experience, these can be best managed in school. A similar approach can be used by a teacher approaching a parent with concerns about a child. Teachers don't like being told what to do by parents, just as parents often resent being told what to do by teachers! Seeking the help of the other sets the scene for mutual cooperation aimed at helping the child.

In rare instances, parents may react very defensively when a teacher or school guidance counsellor raises concern about their child's anxiety with them. They may deny there is any problem or blame the school for causing it. This situation requires sensitive handling.

BOBBY'S STORY

Bobby, aged 13, dreaded Wednesdays, as he had a double period of football training on that day. He felt he was 'useless' at football, but the big problem was having to change into his football gear in front of the other boys, as he had not yet started to develop the way some of them had and he felt he must be 'abnormal'. He developed a pattern of feeling sick on Wednesday mornings and having to miss school. It took a number of weeks before he was able to tell his mum about his worries.

Initially, Bobby's mum did not know how to approach this. She knew that football training was compulsory and that the sports coach, Mr Wilson, was known to have a 'no nonsense' way with the boys and their parents. Her initial response was to write a 'sick note' for Bobby for a number of Wednesdays. She would have liked to have him excused from football training completely but knew this could only be done with a doctor's letter. Having given it some thought, she made an appointment to see Mr Wilson and explained the situation to him, asking him how best he thought it could be managed. To her surprise, Mr Wilson said he had dealt with situations like this many times, and in his experience it would be best if Bobby continued football but that he could come to school on Wednesdays with his football gear on under his tracksuit. He would introduce this option for the whole class, as he thought it likely that other boys also found public changing difficult.

This new arrangement worked well. Bobby was still not happy about having to do football, but he was able to attend football on Wednesdays. His mum checked in with Mr Wilson after a few weeks, to thank him for his help and was told that Bobby was making good progress at football. She told Bobby this, but he was not impressed!

Not all teachers have Mr Brown's experience and flexibility. If it is not possible to find a workable solution with the class teacher, it may be necessary to approach the year head, explaining the situation and seeking their help in finding a way to manage it. Very occasionally, if the problem is proving to be very difficult to deal with and good communication cannot be achieved, it may be necessary to seek a different school for the child, but with effort on both sides this is rarely needed.

ACADEMIC PROBLEMS

Young people with problematic anxiety may have academic problems for many reasons. Their school attendance may be poor due to anxiety; homework tasks may take much longer than necessary as they perceive their work to be not good enough; or they may become so anxious about a subject with which they have difficulty that they either avoid it and fall behind or become consumed with it to the detriment of other subjects. They dislike being singled out for special attention in any way, whether it is to read aloud or being selected for special privileges or projects. If discussion is needed about their academic progress, this is best done out of class time, which may need a creative approach by the teacher.

Anxiety can lead to difficulty with concentration, which may make it appear that the young person is not trying. If there is a change in the young person's normal performance, an astute teacher may wonder what lies behind it. Discussion with the young person and their parent may help to clarify matters. When a young person is struggling academically, an experienced teacher who knows the young person well is usually the best person to advise on whether an educational assessment is needed to clarify if the child may have a general or specific learning difficulty, and they will know how this can be arranged.

Anxious children often spend far too long on homework, either due to concentration problems or concerns that it is not good enough. This may lead to conflict at home with frustrated parents, which adds to the child's anxiety. An agreement with the teacher about a reasonable amount of time for homework should help with this situation. Young people with obsessive compulsive disorder (OCD), a specific anxiety disorder, often spend excessive amounts of time on homework, checking and rechecking it, or repeating assignments. Please see Chapter 6 for further information about helping with OCD.

Anxiety focused on a particular teacher

What is the best way to respond when a young person's anxiety is focused on one particular teacher? It is important to find out from the young person as much as possible about their interaction with the teacher, but this should be done in a spirit of interested curiosity, rather than appearing to be 'gathering evidence'. It is important not to speak negatively about the teacher in front of the young person, as this is unhelpful and may make the situation for the young person even more difficult. It is sometimes useful to seek the views informally of other parents whom you trust about their experience of the teacher, but again this should be done in a low-key way. An approach such as, 'Ben does not seem to be happy in school at the moment. How is your Pete finding things?' will yield the information you need without suggesting a problem with the teacher.

Children who say they hate their teacher are often repeating what they have heard their peers say and may not have a particular problem with the teacher. But if the child's anxiety about the teacher is interfering with their school work or making school attendance difficult, it is important to talk to the teacher. An appointment needs to be arranged outside of class time. This may be difficult, but if approached calmly, in the spirit of seeking the teacher's help rather than pointing the finger, it can be very useful. 'Ben does not seem too happy in school at the moment. I am wondering if you have noticed it? Have you any ideas about how best to help him?' Conversations like this can avoid either teacher or parent becoming defensive and feeling blamed. It is a good idea to plan a follow-up meeting, so that each can give the other feedback about how things are going for the child.

If these meetings fail to resolve the problem and the child continues to be affected by significant anxiety related to the teacher, the next step is to seek a meeting with the year head or principal. This should be approached in the same way as outlined above, with the aim of seeking guidance on how best to help the child. A calm approach while giving the principal an account of the problem with the child, and of the meetings with the teacher and their outcome, is essential. If a meeting such as this does not lead to improvement, a request for the child to change class can be made. This is rarely popular with schools, for administrative and other reasons, and may be impossible. The next step is a decision to change school, which may help. Parents know their child best and should give this careful thought, as a child whose anxiety is holding them back in one school may well carry that problem through to the next school. It may be more helpful to try to get through the academic year with the teacher with whom they had a problem, using some of the ideas from Chapter 3 on how to help the young person manage their anxiety. Success with this would give the child confidence and would be an invaluable learning experience for future coping with a difficult relationship.

SOCIAL PROBLEMS

While many anxious children have one or two close friends and are content with this, some avoid interaction with peers and are shy and withdrawn. Others, in their anxiety to have a friend, are overly intrusive and clingy, which puts peers off. While parents of very young children can arrange 'play dates' and can prepare the child for these, this becomes more difficult as the child gets older. A parent cannot actively make friends for their child, but they can help in a number of other ways. They can build up the child's confidence by noticing and commenting positively when the child makes an attempt to handle a social situation. They can observe their child with peers, thus getting an idea of where the difficulty lies and they can use rehearsal and role play to help. This can be done in a fun way if the child is cooperative, but many anxious children are highly sensitive about their social difficulties and resist parents' or teachers' attempts to talk about them or intervene in any way. Persisting with trying to get the child to talk about such problems makes them more anxious, as they pick up on the adult's anxiety. With such children, it works better to help them become more socially confident by praising everyday activities such as answering the phone, buying something in a shop, greeting a neighbour or conveying a message in school. Helping someone else has been shown to be very beneficial for both adults and children with anxiety, and some anxious children blossom with being asked to be a 'buddy' to another anxious child.

Avoiding children being left out

Teachers of primary school children can do much to avoid children being consistently picked last or left out of team games by randomly giving each child a number and then allocating all the even numbers to one team and the odd ones to the other. Intervening in the playground is more difficult and probably less helpful. Many anxious children dread the unstructured nature of the playground and the prospect of standing alone while others play happily. Some schools address this by having an area where quieter children can congregate around a particular interest, such as chess or board games. Some schools also address the problem of 'not being asked to birthday parties', which can cause such pain for children, by suggesting that parents of children whose birthdays are near each other might team up and hold a joint birthday party to which the whole class is invited. While this may involve the cost of hiring a venue, it often works out cheaper than each parent hosting a party.

BULLYING

Bullying seems to be a universal social problem at all stages of life, despite the widespread presence of anti-bullying policies. Many schools have excellent anti-bullying policies that are rigorously enforced and everyone is aware that the ethos of the school ensures that bullying is taken very seriously. Unfortunately, this is not the case in all schools. In an Irish survey, about 30 per cent of primary school students and 16 per cent of secondary school students reported having been bullied at some time (O'Moore 1997), while a further Irish survey involving more than 10,000 children showed that 16.5 per cent of school-aged children (22% of boys and 10% of girls) reported having bullied others in the past couple of months (Callaghan and The HBSC Ireland Team 2012). These statistics are similar in most Western cultures.

Anxious children are vulnerable to being bullied, as they tend not to fight back and often do not have a protective network of friends. It is often difficult to know whether the anxiety or the bullying came first, but they tend to feed off each other and get into a vicious cycle.

LINDA'S STORY

'The last year at school has been really difficult. I was coming home upset and I wasn't eating as much, and my mam was really worried about me. The girls in my class were really, really mean to me. I was paranoid going into school every morning about what would happen that day. It was kind of bullying, except I wasn't hit or anything, mostly just being mean. I'd try not to listen to them, like I'd ignore them completely. My mam helped me a lot through that year – though I sometimes lashed out at her, she was always there for me.'

How best to help if you suspect that a young person is being bullied is not always clear-cut. They will rarely tell you about it, and while physical bullying may be easier to spot, psychological bullying is much more difficult. Many young people are relentlessly teased, ignored, excluded or subjected to nasty texts, emails or messages on Facebook and never tell anyone about it. Part of the reason for not telling is the erosion of self-esteem that bullying causes, whereby the victim starts to believe they are in some way responsible, and a fear that 'telling' may make the situation even worse. They also may fear that their access to the Internet may be blocked.

It is important to try to talk to the young person, but asking directly, 'Are you being bullied?' is likely to get an angry, negative response. It seems to work better if you mention what you have noticed, such as, 'I've noticed you seem upset when you come home from school. Is there anyway I can help?' This is also likely to get a response such as, 'I'm fine', but you have sown the seeds for the possibility that the young person may talk to you later. If they do, remaining calm is the key – simply listen to what the young person has to say, make it clear you understand how hurtful it must be for them and find out what they would like to happen. They always want the bullying to stop but usually in a way that does not involve 'telling tales' or being 'a rat'. While your instinct may be to instantly 'name names' and demand that the school take steps to punish the culprits, this is rarely what the young person wants and may be impossible anyway, as much cyberbullying is anonymous and difficult to track down. It is better to consider simple steps initially, such as discussing with the young person the importance of not responding to offensive messages, not retaliating by becoming a cyberbully themselves (young people often flip in and out of the bully–victim role) and possibly agreeing to have no electronic communication devices in their bedroom at night. There is useful information on the Internet about dealing with cyberbullying (see www.reachout.com). It is possible to report or block offensive input to social networking sites or mobile phones and to get sites shut down. This sounds straightforward, but in practice it tends to be difficult and requires experience, confidence and persistence. Threatening messages may need to be reported to the police, who will advise on what needs to be done.

Schools have an important role to play in the prevention of bullying but need to work with young people and their parents to create an ethos where bullying is less likely to happen. School can be a haven for many young people with problematic anxiety, with its structure and familiarity, but it needs vigilance on the part of parents and teachers to make sure it is a 'safe haven'.

CHAPTER **5**

HELPING WITH COMMON FORMS OF ANXIETY

Generalized anxiety, panic attacks, separation anxiety and phobias are some of the most common forms of anxiety in young people. This chapter gives parents and teachers information about these difficulties and how to recognize and manage them.

Most of us are familiar with anxiety and have experienced it ourselves at various times in our lives. As adults, we tend to know ourselves well enough to be able to understand what has caused us to be anxious and to realize that, no matter how bad it is at a particular time, it tends not to last. But young people do not have this life experience and can become overwhelmed with feelings they do not understand, which makes them feel 'not normal'. The stigma that still surrounds mental health problems means that few people of any age who are currently experiencing such difficulties confide in others, sometimes not even those closest to them. If they were able to talk openly about their experience, they might realize how common anxiety problems are, and some of the burden of feeling 'not normal' might be lifted.

Young people who have anxiety disorders rarely recognize this for themselves. They are aware of their feelings and experiences but don't know why they feel as they do and often fear they are 'going mad'. They are dependent on the adults around them to help them make sense of what they are experiencing and to support them in coping.

WHEN DOES ORDINARY ANXIETY BECOME A 'DISORDER'?

When anxiety is severe and persistent, causing significant distress and interfering with the person's ability to function in everyday life, it is considered an anxiety disorder. Sometimes anxiety disorders come on 'out of the blue' in someone who has not had previous problems with anxiety, but more often they occur in people who have previously been prone to anxiety. This sometimes happens at times of change in their lives or when they are experiencing relationship or other difficulties, but sometimes there is no obvious trigger for worsening anxiety. Anxiety disorders are categorized by mental health professionals into different types, but there is much overlap between them and there are many similarities in how best to manage and treat them.

RECOGNIZING GENERALIZED ANXIETY DISORDERS (GADS)

Young people with GADs have severe and persistent anxiety that greatly affects their lives. They worry a great deal and often have a constant feeling of dread, which they cannot pinpoint to anything in particular. They may look pale and stressed and often have difficulty sleeping. Relaxation is very difficult and they are often restless, irritable and 'edgy'. Headaches, aches and pains and a general feeling of being unwell are common. Everyday situations, such as going to school, answering the phone, doing homework or going shopping, which they have previously managed without difficulty, may become very challenging. They have difficulty concentrating, and their school work may deteriorate. Social situations become highly anxiety provoking, and they may withdraw from friends and even sometimes from family. They find uncertainty particularly hard to handle and may seek constant reassurance.

If you suspect that a young person has an anxiety disorder, it is a good idea to bring them to the GP for a check-up. There are two reasons for doing this. First, the doctor will check their physical health to ensure there is no underlying physical cause for their anxiety. Very occasionally, conditions such as an overactive thyroid gland, an abnormal heart rhythm or low blood sugar can cause anxiety-like symptoms. Second, it can be very reassuring to the young person to be given a definite diagnosis of an anxiety disorder from a doctor who can explain how common such disorders are, that they are not 'going mad' and how such disorders can be helped.

CLAUDIA'S STORY

Claudia, aged 14, and her family were due to move house to a different town, as her father had got a new job. She had always been a worrier, but as the move got nearer, she became more and more anxious. She could not sleep alone and begged her parents to allow her to sleep in their bedroom, which they reluctantly agreed to, hoping it would be temporary. She constantly sought reassurance from her mother about the move, asking whether she would make friends, like the new school and be able to keep in contact with her old friends. She refused to stay in the house on her own, which meant that her mother had to take time off from her part-time job. Everyone in the family was affected by

Claudia's anxiety. Her two older brothers called her 'mad' and 'a loser'. When this happened she became very angry, screaming, crying and barricading herself in her bedroom. There were frequent arguments between her parents. Her mother, who had suffered from anxiety herself in the past, felt sorry for her, but also felt angry, while her father felt she needed a 'firm hand' and urged her mother to 'be stricter' with her but was unable to do this himself. The family was in turmoil.

SELF-HELP TIPS FOR YOUNG PEOPLE WITH GADS

In addition to the ideas outlined in Chapter 3, there is much that young people with GADs can do to help themselves.

Talking to someone who can help

Encouraging a young person to talk about how they are feeling may be more difficult than it sounds. Children often welcome the opportunity to talk, but teenagers often do not want adults (particularly those close to them) to 'get inside their heads'. A low-key approach seems to work best – a simple comment or statement such as, 'I notice you seem a bit hassled today; is there any way I can help?', or, 'I am here if you would like to talk – you look as if you have had a tough day.'

Having useful information about anxiety disorders

Young people live in a world bombarded with information from various sources, but often do not have good information about mental health issues. Despite the existence of some excellent websites such as www.reachout.com and www.youngminds.org.uk, which feature real young people telling their stories of having a mental health problem, how they coped and what helped, it is not clear how much young people in difficulties actually use them. It is worth looking at some of the online resources listed in the Appendix of this book, and, if you feel they may be useful, to mention to the young person that you came across something about anxiety that they may find interesting.

Building exercise and relaxation into their lives

There are many research studies that show that exercise has a beneficial effect on anxiety (Carek, Laibstain and Carek 2011; Otto and Smits 2011). Some even show that exercise can be as effective as medication in the treatment of mild to moderate levels of anxiety. Building some form of exercise into the young person's daily routine is good for their general health, and when they are exercising they are likely to be distracted from worrying. Football, tennis, netball, hockey, rugby, martial arts, boxing and dance are some examples of forms of exercise that have the additional advantage of involving interaction with others. Young people who prefer more solitary forms of exercise, such as running or going to the gym, can still benefit from the distraction and sense of mastery that such activities can bring. Parents sometimes find that young people who are not prepared to exercise on their own will join them in activities that they can do together, such as dance classes, yoga, pilates or even taking the dog for a walk.

Relaxation techniques have been shown in some studies to be as effective as some forms of therapy in the treatment of anxiety (Arntz 2003), and there are many guides to relaxation techniques available on the Internet and on DVD. Some schools have introduced yoga into the curriculum and have found that it appeals to the students and benefits classroom behaviour and learning.

Meditation and mindfulness

These approaches have become popular in recent years. They help young people to live in the present moment and to be less fearful of bodily sensations. In my experience, young people with severe anxiety find it very difficult to learn these skills, and are unable to relax enough to practise them. However, with an experienced, sympathetic and encouraging teacher, many can manage to do so and can benefit greatly from the resulting sense of being able to do something to help themselves.

Postponing worrying

Part of 'externalizing the problem' (see Chapter 3) can involve the young person deciding to put off worrying about a particular problem for a specified period of time, maybe starting with something manageable like 15 minutes and building up gradually to several hours. This gives them a sense of control, and when the time comes to start worrying again, the 'power' has often gone from the worry and they are able to view it differently.

Taking small steps

Problems that are overwhelming become much more manageable when broken down into small steps that are taken one at a time. For example, an older adolescent who is unable to be in the house on their own due to anxiety could be encouraged to remain home alone for five or ten minutes initially, gradually increasing the time over a number of weeks.

Listening to music

Many young people say that listening to music helps with their anxiety, and there is some research evidence to support this (Chian *et al.* 2013). The concentration and sense of physical release involved in playing music can also help.

Drama and acting

Some anxious young people blossom in drama classes. They are able to 'stand outside themselves' and enjoy portraying a completely different persona from their usual selves. They can also sometimes use the skills they have learned in such classes to 'act as if not anxious' in handling anxiety-provoking situations. This gives them a sense of mastery and control.

Self-help approaches only work if the young person is prepared to try them out and stick with them. Parents and teachers can make suggestions and give ideas, but they cannot make young people try them, nor can they follow the approaches for them. Repeatedly exhorting young people to try different approaches gives the message that you are anxious about them, which tends to make their anxiety worse. Finding the balance between making a suggestion and 'nagging' can be tricky, and a low-key approach generally works best.

PANIC ATTACKS

A full-blown panic attack is an extremely frightening experience. It usually comes on 'out of the blue' and involves a feeling of intense fear, with a rapid pounding heart, difficulty breathing and a sense of unreality during which the person often fears they are dying. The experience is so distressing that, having experienced one panic attack, the young person may become so fearful of having another that it impacts greatly on their lives. Panic attacks can happen to people who have no previous history of problems with anxiety, but they are much more common in those with such a history. They are usually short lived, rarely lasting longer than ten minutes, but are so intense that it may take the person some time longer to feel 'normal'. They are not uncommon – about 3 per cent of people have experienced at least one panic attack in their lives (American Psychiatric Association 1994). Many people who have had a panic attack can remember it vividly, but their lives were not significantly affected by it. When panic attacks occur frequently and are having a big effect on the person's life, they are referred to as panic disorder.

Full-blown panic attacks are fairly common. Even more common are episodes of 'panic', which are less intense than a full-blown attack but are nonetheless frightening. These usually involve a feeling of increasing fear, increased heart rate and rapid, shallow breathing, accompanied by tingling in the hands and feet and a sensation of being unable to get enough air.

Because panic attacks are so frightening, people who have experienced them often avoid situations where they think they might have another one or from which they would not be easily able to escape if they felt mounting anxiety. This may lead them to limit their lives; they may avoid crowded places, the cinema, shopping centres, lifts, queues, and so forth. In severe cases it may lead to agoraphobia, in which they only feel safe in their own homes.

SELF-HELP TIPS FOR YOUNG PEOPLE WITH PANIC ATTACKS
Understanding anxiety and panic attacks
Understanding what is happening during a panic attack helps some young people to feel more in control. While people often feel as if they are going to die during a panic

attack, this does not happen and they can be reassured that they will not die.

Many of the frightening sensations experienced during a panic attack are due to the rapid, shallow breathing brought on by anxiety. This type of breathing results in the lungs blowing off too much carbon dioxide, which leads to chemical imbalances in the blood, leading to the tingling sensations, dizziness and light headedness. These sensations in turn make the person feel more anxious, and their breathing becomes even more rapid and shallow, and the cycle continues.

Slowing down their breathing

Rapid, shallow breathing often precedes, and is very much part of, a panic attack. This type of breathing is called 'hyperventilation'. To counteract it, the young person can slow their breathing by placing their hand on their lower abdomen, focusing on it and breathing in slowly while they count to five, noticing how their hand rises slightly, and then breathing out slowly to the count of five. This will usually need some adult encouragement and supervision initially, but older children and adolescents can learn to do this on their own when they notice their anxiety levels rising.

Using a paper bag

Using a paper bag to treat hyperventilation is an old-fashioned remedy but one that is still widely used. It involves the young person holding a paper bag over their mouth and nose and taking five to ten normal breaths with it in place, and then removing it and taking another five to ten normal breaths, and repeating this cycle until their symptoms have improved and their breathing has slowed down. It is thought to work by ensuring that the person re-breathes the carbon dioxide in their expired air, which helps to restore the chemical imbalance in the blood. It is important not to use a plastic bag.

Young people who have successfully managed a panic attack using this method are often reassured by carrying around a small paper bag with them. Just knowing they have the means to control a panic attack seems to make it less likely to happen. Some therapists would frown on this approach, as it does involve engaging in risk-reducing behaviour, which may be seen as pathological. However, I cannot see much difference between this behaviour and the behaviour of someone who is prone to asthma carrying around an inhaler.

SEPARATION ANXIETY DISORDER

Separation anxiety is a normal part of development in babies and toddlers (see Chapter 1), and in older children often happens at times of change or upheaval in their lives. The key feature is anxiety that is reduced or prevented by the presence of a familiar figure. It is only called a disorder when it occurs in older children and adolescents, is severe and is interfering significantly in the young person's life or development. Separation anxiety disorder commonly results in being unable to sleep alone, being unable to remain at home alone or having difficulty leaving the house or meeting people unless a parent is present. School refusal is often due to separation anxiety disorder (please see Chapter 8). Sometimes it occurs on its own, but often there are other manifestations of anxiety, such as GADs, panic disorder or OCD.

Separation anxiety disorder may lead to negative, oppositional behaviour, temper tantrums, screaming and even physical aggression. This is particularly common in young children but may occur in teenagers. This type of behaviour is often not recognized as being due to separation anxiety disorder; the child is simply regarded as being 'bold' or 'difficult'. An angry reaction on the part of the adults involved often makes the child more anxious. Remaining calm and understanding that anxiety lies behind the young person's difficult behaviour can prevent an escalating cycle of negative behaviour.

SELF-HELP TIPS FOR YOUNG PEOPLE WITH SEPARATION ANXIETY DISORDER

With young children who are being left with a responsible adult with whom they are familiar, a brief explanation that you will be back, a suggestion of something interesting they might do when you are gone and a quick, decisive departure are important. Parents, in their anxiety to soothe their screaming child, often delay their departure while attempting to reassure their child. This rarely works and usually makes separation even more difficult. Knowing that you can trust the person minding your child to contact you if your child does not settle is reassuring, as separation anxiety is often a two-way issue.

Teenagers with separation anxiety disorder are often acutely aware of missing out on experiences they wish they could enjoy, such as meeting friends, sleepovers and school trips. Many of the tips for managing GADs are useful and may encourage them to try a programme of managing gradually increasing time separated from their familiar figure. For example, a teenager who is only able to relax when at home with a parent could agree to walk to the gate on day one, to the postbox on day two, to the nearest shops on day three and further afield with each successive day. They will need to be encouraged to 'boss back' the anxiety this will involve and have a plan for managing it. Their anxiety levels usually fall as their confidence and sense of achievement rise with this approach.

PHOBIAS

A phobia is an intense, persistent and irrational fear of an object, activity or situation. People with phobias tend to take complicated steps to avoid the feared object or situation. Phobias are very common and usually do not interfere with the person's life. They only become problematic if they are particularly severe or if they are causing significant distress or limiting the person's lifestyle. For example, many young children are afraid of 'monsters'. For most, this just shows itself in them saying they are afraid and maybe avoiding certain TV programmes and computer games that feature scary monsters. For others, their fear of monsters is so severe that they are constantly on high alert in case a monster should appear, seek constant reassurance that there are no monsters about and become unable to sleep in case they dream of monsters.

Agoraphobia is a fear of open areas, crowds or public places, leading the person to only feel safe in their own home. It sometimes develops in people who have panic attacks but may occur without any history of panic attacks. It is unusual in small children but often has its onset in adolescence.

Few children like 'getting needles', but manage immunizations, injections and dental appointments without too many problems. For children with needle phobia, these procedures become very difficult or impossible, and professional help is often needed. Most children's hospitals have psychologists with experience of treating needle phobia.

SELF-HELP TIPS FOR YOUNG PEOPLE WITH PHOBIAS

Phobias only need special attention if they are interfering with the young person's life and preventing them doing things they would like to do. Many of the ideas given already can help, in particular talking to someone who is able to provide help, having information about anxiety and phobias and slowing down breathing. There is much research that the most effective treatment for phobias is gradual exposure to the feared object or situation. This is the approach most likely to be used with young people who are attending a professional for help with phobias. There is excellent information and a step-by-step guide to using this approach on a useful Canadian website (www.anxietybc.com). Gradual exposure needs the support of a calm, patient, confident and encouraging adult, who the young person trusts. Some parents successfully manage this approach with their young person, but many feel they are too emotionally involved and prefer to seek professional help.

The ideas in this chapter can help young people to manage their anxiety themselves, which gives them a sense of achievement and control. Should professional help be needed for more severe anxiety problems, much of this will involve the professional working with the young person to help them try these ideas for themselves.

CHAPTER 6

HELPING WITH DIFFERENT TYPES OF ANXIETY

This chapter describes the many guises anxiety can take and gives information about how best to deal with them. Anxiety may be associated with depression, self-harm, behaviour difficulties, attention deficit hyperactivity disorder, autistic spectrum disorders, selective mutism, anorexia nervosa, tics and obsessive compulsive disorder – all of which are helped greatly by parents and teachers who are informed about how best to respond.

Anxiety can occur on its own, but it is often associated with other mental health problems. Having information about these problems will help parents and teachers to respond in ways that are most helpful for the young person.

DEPRESSION

Anxiety and depression often co-exist in young people, and many researchers believe they are all part of the same underlying disorder. Depression in young people shows itself in a lowering of mood or loss of interest in things that were previously enjoyed, often associated with irritability, sleep disturbance, appetite changes, poor concentration, unexplained physical symptoms, feelings of worthlessness and thoughts of death or suicidal thoughts or acts. Many of these symptoms overlap with those of anxiety, and it can be difficult to pick them apart. Where anxiety co-exists with depression, it often takes the form of excessive worrying about the future and rumination (the experience of constantly and repeatedly going over thoughts of negative experiences).

MEGAN'S STORY

Megan, aged 15, has always been a quiet, conscientious girl, who worked hard at school and had a small group of friends. In recent months, she has become more withdrawn and seems to have fallen out with most of her friends. She has given up netball, saying she is no good at it, and, despite spending long periods in her room apparently doing her homework, she is struggling to keep up with her school work.

Her teachers cannot understand why she is 'not trying', but Megan feels she is trying as hard as she can. She worries that she will fail her forthcoming exams, and seems preoccupied with her health. She has been to the family doctor three times in the past four months with a variety of aches and pains, but the doctor has found nothing wrong.

Megan lives with her mother and always had a good relationship with her until recently. Now she is irritable and bad-tempered, and her mother cannot understand what is the matter with her. When she asks Megan if anything is wrong, Megan angrily replies that she is 'fine' and walks out of the room.

Continued on page 63.

Depression can range from being a mild problem, which responds to adult support and self-help measures, to a severe one, where professional help is needed. Advice on how to decide if professional help is needed is given in Chapter 7.

SELF-HARM

Self-harm is a common problem in young people. A number of community-based studies have shown that about 10 per cent of young people have engaged in acts of self-harm (Hawton *et al.* 2002; Sullivan *et al.* 2004). Only a tiny fraction of these have come to medical attention, and often no one except the young person has known about the self-harm. Self-harm can involve a variety of behaviours, such as cutting oneself, taking an overdose of tablets, banging your head or fist against a wall or attempting to strangle or hang oneself. Occasionally such behaviours are deliberate suicide attempts, but more often they are acts that the young person engages in to get relief from unbearable emotional pain. Such young people sometimes explain that the physical pain from harming themselves is easier to cope with than their mental pain.

Self-harm may involve a single episode, carried out at a time when the young person is feeling 'at rock bottom' or it may be repeated. In a small number of cases, it is repeated regularly and can become a habit that is hard to break.

MEGAN'S STORY

Continued from page 62.
One evening, when Megan is in the kitchen getting something to eat, her mother notices what look like cuts on her forearm. When she enquires about it, Megan says that a friend's cat scratched her. When further cuts appear some weeks later, Megan's mother becomes concerned

and feels she has to talk to Megan. She realizes that Megan is likely to become angry, as she has done before when her mother has tried to talk to her about how she is feeling. She plans how she will bring up the subject with Megan and chooses a time when she is calm and Megan is in relatively good form. She does not ask Megan directly about the cuts, but simply says she has noticed them and that she knows that sometimes people cut themselves when they are very upset. She says that she is there if Megan wants to talk, or that she can arrange for her to see a counsellor if Megan would prefer that.

Megan does not reply, and leaves the room, but not in the angry way that she has responded in the past. A few days later, she asks her mother to arrange for her to see someone she could talk to, saying she has been feeling 'a bit down' recently.

BEHAVIOUR DIFFICULTIES

Negative, hostile or oppositional behaviour may be fuelled by underlying anxiety. In these situations, it is often not recognized that anxiety is a driving force. Such behaviour tends to push others away and can be so hard to take and hurtful that few people are willing to consider what may be driving it. It is not difficult to empathize and be patient with a three-year-old with separation anxiety who is screaming, kicking and clinging because they do not want to be left, but similar behaviour in a 13-year-old with separation anxiety tends to lead to angry responses from others, which often make things worse. Dealing with such situations needs endless patience and a determination to try to understand the young person and to keep a connection with them.

ATTENTION DEFICIT HYPERACTIVITY DISORDER (ADHD)

About 30 per cent of young people with ADHD also suffer from problematic anxiety (Biederman, Newcorn and Sprich 1991). Possible reasons why these two disorders may co-exist include genetic factors, as well as the experiences of being overwhelmed, of repeated failure and of not living up to the expectations of others, which are so common in young people with ADHD. Helping such young people involves making sure their ADHD is recognized and treated effectively, and helping them to manage their anxiety using the ideas discussed in previous chapters. While medication for ADHD can be very effective, occasionally some of the medications may lead to worsening of anxiety symptoms. If there is concern that this may be happening, it should be discussed with the doctor who is prescribing and monitoring the young person's medication.

There are many useful websites for people with ADHD and their parents, carers and teachers, including: www.adhdandyou.com and www.addiss.co.uk.

AUTISTIC SPECTRUM DISORDERS

Young people with autistic spectrum disorders are very susceptible to anxiety for many reasons. Their communication and social difficulties make it very hard for them to understand what is happening around them and make it difficult for adults to reassure them. Their sensory processing difficulties may lead them to experience events and sensations in a very different way, so experiences that we may assume to be pleasurable may be highly upsetting for them. A useful document, 'Managing Anxiety in the Classroom', is available from www.middletownautism.com/research. While this is primarily for teachers of young people with autistic spectrum disorders, it contains much useful advice that can be used at home. It gives guidance on reducing unpredictability, creating a sense of calmness and avoiding sensory overload.

SELECTIVE MUTISM

This intriguing condition is rare in its full-blown form but lesser degrees are more common. It is characterized by a persistent failure to speak in certain situations where speaking is expected, while speaking normally in other situations. It is a little more common in girls than in boys and usually comes to light sometime after the child starts school, although some failure to speak in social situations may have been present long before that. Children with selective mutism typically do not speak in school, while speaking normally within the family. They can communicate non-verbally, although some children who are particularly anxious may appear expressionless and motionless in social situations. It is probably a type of extreme social anxiety.

Children with selective mutism engender great frustration in adults, who know they can speak but sometimes feel they are deliberately choosing not to. Understanding that severe anxiety is preventing the child from speaking may help to reduce frustration and to appreciate that the more pressure that is put on the child to speak, the less likely they are to do so.

When starting school, many shy children take a considerable time to speak with ease. However, if a child who is speaking with ease at home has not spoken at all to the teacher after several months, it is worth trying a simple reward system to encourage the child to speak. This would involve the parent making a simple sticker chart and explaining to the child that they will ask the teacher to let them know if the child said any words that day. The parent will have already practised some simple phrases with the child, such as 'yes, please' and 'no, thank you'. If the child does speak to the teacher, the parent lets the child choose a sticker to put on the chart and will have agreed with the child what treat they will get when they have a certain number of stickers. It is important that the treats are small and repeatable so they can be given for a very small number of stickers. An approach such as this needs to be carried out very calmly by parent and teacher, who need to work closely together. If it has not worked after a week or two, it should be discontinued and can be tried again after another few months.

If the child is still not speaking in school by the end of the first year, referral for professional help is indicated. This will usually be to a clinical psychologist with experience of working with young children and their families, but some areas have multidisciplinary teams of professionals who provide this service. Such teams often include clinical psychologists, speech and language therapists and occupational therapists. With treatment, most children with selective mutism become less anxious and able to speak outside the family, but some remain shy and socially anxious into the teenage years.

ANOREXIA NERVOSA

Anorexia nervosa is a condition in which the young person's anxiety is totally focused on fear of fatness, which leads them to take drastic steps to pursue thinness. They reduce their food intake and often over-exercise. When their body weight falls below a certain critical level, their periods stop or the onset of periods is delayed in those who are pre-pubertal. It usually starts in adolescence, and is more common in girls, but boys can also be affected. The young person's thinking becomes distorted, leading them to see themselves as 'fat', while others see someone whose weight loss is frightening.

Anorexia nervosa is a serious condition, as the food restriction and weight loss can lead to dangerous changes in the body, some of which may have long-term consequences and may occasionally lead to death. It is usually extremely difficult to persuade the young person to accept help, as their distorted thinking leads them to believe that their behaviour is the only way they can manage their feelings of emotional turmoil. It takes great determination on the part of parents, carers and mental health professionals to get them to accept the help they need, but most do so eventually. An excellent book called *Helping Your Teenager Beat an Eating Disorder* (Lock and Le Grange 2005) gives invaluable information and support to parents, enabling them to have the confidence to temporarily take charge of their teenager's eating, while ensuring they get the professional help they need.

TICS

Tics are involuntary, sudden, repetitive, rapid movements (motor tics) or sounds (phonic tics), which are quite common in children, especially in boys. They usually involve simple movements like blinking or shoulder shrugging and sounds such as throat clearing, coughing or clicking. Sometimes the tics are more complex, involving jumping, twirling or uttering phrases. Most tics are transient; they come and go over weeks to months and eventually disappear. Some, however, are more chronic. The combination of motor and phonic tics that last more than a year is referred to as Tourette's disorder.

Tics have a strong genetic basis and are not caused by anxiety. However, anxiety can make them worse. While they are involuntary, some children can control them for a period of time. Sometimes they can be suppressed while the child is in school, but are then 'released' when they get home, at which time they appear particularly bad.

Many children with mild tics are unaware of them, and it is best not to draw attention to them. Tics can sometimes cause problems for the child, usually because of the reaction of others. They are often most noticeable when the child is over-stimulated, so a calm environment helps. Having a quiet area that the child can go to in school if the tics are bad also helps. Being able to talk to someone – a parent or a therapist – about the tics also helps, as it supports the child to understand the disorder and gives them hope for the future.

There are types of cognitive behavioural therapy called 'habit reversal therapy' and 'comprehensive behavioural intervention for tics' that have been shown in some studies to be effective in reducing tics. These therapies are quite hard work and are probably most suitable for teenagers with moderate to severe tics, who have the cognitive ability and motivation to practise them. Medication is usually only considered for tics that are causing significant problems for the child. This is because most of the relevant medications have unwanted side effects. A 'trial-and-error' approach with different medications is often needed before one that suits the particular child is found.

Useful information about tics is available at www.aboutourkids.org and young people with Tourette's disorder can link with one another at www.tourettes-action.org.uk.

OBSESSIVE COMPULSIVE DISORDER (OCD)

It used to be thought that OCD was a rare disorder, but we now know that it is relatively common, occurring in 2–3 per cent of the population. Like most other anxiety disorders, it can range from mild, when it is just a nuisance, to so severe that the person's life is dominated by it. It usually starts in adolescence, but may sometimes affect younger children. It is characterized by the presence of obsessions – unwanted, disturbing, repetitive thoughts, images or impulses that the person often recognizes as illogical but that they cannot stop thinking about – and compulsions – repeated behaviours that the person feels compelled to carry out, often because they feel these behaviours in some way prevent the feared outcome of the obsessions. Common obsessions include fear of contaminating oneself or a loved one, leading to compulsive hand washing, or fear of harm coming to oneself or another through leaving the cooker on or a door unlocked, leading to compulsive checking of switches and locks. Minor anxiety in these areas is very common, but in people with OCD such preoccupations can take up hours every day and lead to great distress in the sufferer and in family members. The obsessions are sometimes of a sexual or violent nature, which are very much out of character for the young person and which they find highly disturbing. Young people with OCD often think they are 'going mad' and may take complicated steps to hide their symptoms from others. Others seek help from parents and family members, asking them to check things for them, and many parents, wishing to help their child, become involved in their compulsions.

Many young people with OCD are greatly helped by understanding more about it and by being reassured that they are not 'going mad'. Having information helps them to externalize the problem and may give them the motivation to practise some of the self-help tips described in Chapters 3 and 5. Some approaches that are particularly useful are listed here.

Thinking differently

Young people with OCD who understand the disorder may be able to think differently and view their obsessions and compulsions not as an intrinsic part of themselves that indicates that they are 'mad', but rather as being due to a fairly common disorder that can be managed. Often the use of self-talk helps with this. When an obsession comes into their head, they are able to say to themselves, 'This is just the OCD – I can manage it.' The feeling of being able to control OCD rather than be controlled by it helps restore their confidence and sense of mastery.

Postponing obsessions and compulsions

With increasing confidence, young people with OCD may be prepared to try delaying focusing on their obsessions or carrying out compulsive behaviour. For example, a young person with compulsive checking may take an hour to make their bed in the morning, as they feel compelled to straighten every wrinkle and tuck in the sheets in a neat and symmetrical way. One day they might decide that they will just throw up the duvet and defer the checking for 15 minutes. Often compulsions are not as strong when deferred, and they may find they are able to defer the behaviour for a further 15 minutes. Even if they cannot defer the behaviour further, when they do carry it out it tends to be for a shorter time.

Distraction

Anything that helps to distract from obsessions and compulsions is worth pursuing, such as listening to music, exercising, writing or connecting with peers on social media.

Parents and carers can help by not becoming involved in arguments about the obsessions and compulsions. There is no point in trying to convince someone with OCD that the chance of contaminating someone is minimal. Their concerns are not logical, and their failure to respond to reassurance leads to increasing frustration all round. It is better to help externalize the OCD by responding to requests to become involved by calmly saying something like, 'I'm sorry, but that is just your OCD getting at you.'

This often results in the young person pleading and becoming more upset, angry and demanding, but getting involved in their compulsions only leads to the OCD becoming more entrenched and harder to manage.

Young Minds, a respected UK-based mental health charity, has a very useful website (www.youngminds.org.uk) with information about OCD for young people, parents and carers.

KEN'S STORY

Ken, aged 14, had severe OCD. It took him hours to get ready for school in the mornings, as he had to do everything, such as showering, dressing, and eating breakfast, in a particular order and to a particular standard. If he departed from his routine, or did not do something quite right, he had to start that activity again. He had to be ready for the school bus at 7.45am, and was getting up earlier and earlier to make it on time. His mother, Maria, had been helping him out by laying out his clothes in the order he required and making his bed to the required standard, which sometimes seemed to help him but often led to conflict between them, as she rarely got it 'right'.

It was only when things had got completely out of hand and Ken was setting his alarm for 4.30am that his parents realized that he and they needed help. It was not easy to persuade Ken to attend the appointment with the psychiatrist, but when he realized that his parents would attend with him, he agreed to go. The first few sessions involved Ken and his parents learning about OCD, how common it is and the type of treatment that helps. The psychiatrist explained that the temporary reduction in anxiety that people with OCD experience when they carry out their compulsions helps to ensure that the compulsions will be repeated. If the person manages to tolerate the anxiety without carrying out the compulsion, they find that the anxiety does not last, and the need to carry out the compulsion lessens with time. Ken agreed to start a course of cognitive behavioural therapy, which helped put this idea into practice. He was not willing to take the selective serotonin reuptake inhibitor (SSRI) medication that the psychiatrist recommended, which has been shown to be of benefit in OCD, but said he might rethink that decision at a future date. His parents decided that they would do their best not to become involved with his compulsions, as they now understood that this was not helpful in the long run.

Recognizing the role that anxiety plays in a variety of mental health disorders can make them easier to understand and can help parents, teachers and carers to support young people in the use of the many self-help techniques that have been shown to be of value.

CHAPTER 7

GETTING PROFESSIONAL HELP

This chapter helps parents and carers to recognize when professional help is needed in addition to their support. It describes how to access the services available and the types of treatment they provide. Different approaches to treatment are outlined, including cognitive behavioural therapy, other types of psychotherapy and family therapy, using the most up-to-date evidence about 'what works with whom'. The role of medication in particular situations is also addressed.

WHEN IS PROFESSIONAL HELP NEEDED?

Anxiety tends to wax and wane, and it can be hard to know when professional help is needed. Acknowledging that anxiety is causing difficulty for the young person can in itself be very helpful and may lead to the use of some of the self-help approaches already described. The following pointers give an idea of when self-help is insufficient and professional help is indicated. Professional help is normally required when:

- the young person's difficulties are causing significant suffering for themselves or the family

- the young person is unable to get on with life because of their difficulties; they may be unable to mix socially or be unable to manage in school

- the young person's health is affected due to their difficulties; for example, they may be unable to sleep, have lost or gained weight to an unhealthy degree or be using drugs or alcohol as a coping mechanism

- there are concerns about self-harm or suicidal behaviour.

FINDING OUT WHAT SERVICES ARE AVAILABLE

An appointment with the family doctor is a good place to start. A supportive GP who is comfortable dealing with young people with anxiety-related difficulties is an invaluable asset. Many young people who are reluctant to attend more formal services will attend their GP, and that support may be sufficient. If additional help is needed, the GP will know what services are available locally and how to access them. Some general practices have counsellors or psychotherapists as part of the service provided, which the GP may recommend.

The school counsellor is another useful possibility. Some schools have had cutbacks in this service in the recent recession, but it is well worth looking into what support can be provided in school. Some young people don't want the school to know they are experiencing difficulties but may be prepared to attend counselling services in their community.

A word of caution about choosing a counsellor or therapist: in many countries, anyone can describe themselves as a counsellor, therapist or psychotherapist, even if they have no related training or qualification. Those employed within public, state-funded services almost always have the required training and qualification, but this is not always the case for those who work exclusively in private practice. Many countries have recognized professional bodies that accredit counsellors and therapists who have appropriate training and qualification, and these bodies have information on their websites about how to find someone suitably trained. The safest way to ensure that the counsellor or therapist who works with your young person is appropriately trained is to get a recommendation from the GP or the school counsellor. At the first meeting with the counsellor or therapist, don't be afraid to ask which professional body they belong to and check that they are on that body's list of registered counsellors or therapists. It sounds quite complicated and it is! Many countries are in the process of establishing state registration for counsellors and therapists, which will help greatly.

Child and adolescent mental health services (CAMHS) are available free of charge to all young people in the UK and Ireland, and most developed countries have similar services, but they may not be free of charge. The GP may recommend such services for those with more complicated or severe anxiety problems or where there are concerns about related difficulties such as self-harm, suicidal behaviour or family difficulties. These services involve teams of mental health professionals, including clinical psychologists, psychiatrists, social workers, family therapists and psychotherapists, which can be very helpful in ensuring that the young person and their family get the specific help they need.

ENCOURAGING THE YOUNG PERSON TO ATTEND

This is straightforward for many young people with anxiety. They know that their life is being affected by their difficulties, and they are happy to go for help. For others, the idea of 'going for help' is so frightening and embarrassing that they refuse and often become angry and defensive when the subject is raised. Often their fear is partly due to lack of information about what 'going for help' involves. As a parent or carer, you can help by being as well informed as you can be about what will be involved. This may mean attending the first appointment without the reluctant young person, to find out what will happen when they do attend. Anxious young people are often reassured by this and by knowing that their parent or carer is also attending, although it is hoped that they will become confident enough to be seen on their own after the first few sessions.

CAMHS have a lot of experience in dealing with young people who find it hard to engage with services. Some have outreach workers who will initially link up with the young person informally, and then, having established a relationship with them, will encourage them to attend the service. This may be needed for a young person whose anxiety is seriously affecting their life.

DIFFERENT APPROACHES TO TREATMENT

There are many different approaches to treatment. Some of these have been evaluated using randomized controlled trials (RCTs), in which young people with anxiety disorders are assessed and then randomly allocated to receive the treatment under study or to a control group, which may involve an alternative treatment or may mean remaining on a waiting list. The outcomes after a fixed period are then compared in the various groups. Treatments that have been shown to be effective using this type of evaluation are called 'evidence-based treatments'. There are many approaches to treatment that have not been evaluated as rigorously, so we cannot say there is an evidence base for them. This does not mean that they do not work – it simply means that we don't have hard evidence to show that they do.

Most types of therapy include what is called 'psychoeducation', which means working with the young person and their family to help them understand anxiety better and how therapy works.

COGNITIVE BEHAVIOURAL THERAPY (CBT)

This is the treatment approach that has the strongest evidence base. It is a very 'user-friendly' type of treatment in which the young person and the therapist work together to help the young person understand how their anxious thoughts, feelings and behaviours feed off one another in a way that makes the anxiety worse. They learn to challenge some of these thoughts, which helps to reduce the anxious feelings and helps them to behave differently. They are encouraged to use coping mechanisms to enable them to manage their anxiety, while taking small but gradually increasing steps to expose themselves to anxiety-provoking situations that they have previously avoided.

One of the advantages of CBT is its short-term nature, most studies having shown that 10 to 20 sessions work well (Compton *et al.* 2004). It is a type of therapy that makes sense to young people and gives them a feeling of being in control, as they set their own goals. It can be done in one-to-one sessions with the therapist or as a group programme, which has the added advantage of reducing their sense of isolation and 'being different'. There are a number of CBT programmes that have a strong evidence base, such as 'Coping Cat', a 16-session programme for children with anxiety, which also involves parents (Kendall and Hedtke 2006). Another is 'Friends for Life,' a group programme that originated in Australia and is now available in many countries, where it is run in schools and clinics. Different versions of the programme are available for different age groups (Barrett and Sonderegger 2005).

Qualified CBT therapists are in short supply in most places, so this type of therapy may not be available. However, many counsellors and therapists now use CBT ideas and principles in their work.

PARENT-DELIVERED CBT

There is exciting research showing that CBT delivered by parents who are shown how to use a CBT manual with their child and are supported by a therapist can be an effective treatment for childhood anxiety disorders (Thirlwall *et al.* 2013). This innovative approach will appeal to many parents and young people and it is hoped it will become widely available.

OTHER TYPES OF PSYCHOTHERAPY AND COUNSELLING

Psychotherapy and counselling are talking therapies, which involve regular meetings between the young person and the therapist. Irrespective of the type of therapy, the relationship between the young person and the therapist – 'the therapeutic relationship' – has been shown to be a very important factor in determining outcome. Interpersonal psychotherapy and psychodynamic psychotherapy have been evaluated and shown to be effective, but there are many types of counselling and psychotherapy that may also be of value, including art, music, play or drama therapy.

FAMILY THERAPY

Family therapy is another evidence-based treatment, which involves a therapist working with as many family members as possible to enable the family to use its strengths to help the young person. People are sometimes a bit wary of family therapy, fearing that they may be scapegoated, or that it will involve 'airing the family's dirty linen' in public. Properly trained family therapists are sensitive to these concerns and work to ensure that therapy is a helpful and positive experience for the family.

EMMA'S STORY

Emma, aged nine, was very nervous when her mother told her they were going to 'see someone' about her worries. She did not really know what that meant. She knew she had lots of worries and that everyone seemed to want her to be different, but she did not think she could be. From the feeling of dread when she woke in the morning until she finally got to sleep at night, her mind was hardly ever free of worrying thoughts. What if she was late for school? Could they run out of petrol on the way? Would she be able to remember the spellings she had learned the night before? Would anyone talk to her at break? Would her mother pick her up on time? Would her dad have a crash in his car? Would her brother tease her again? Her gran was sick – was she going to die? She took hours to get to sleep – would she be too tired tomorrow?

Both of her parents came with her when she went for the appointment. She thought that was very strange, as usually just her mum brought her to the doctor. She worried that things must be very serious for them both to be with her. The lady who saw them in the clinic was called Clare, and she was kind and gentle. Emma was very relieved to have her parents in the room with her, and they answered most of the questions. She thought she would be very embarrassed if she had to see Clare on her own. Clare explained that her job was to help people who had worries and that she would be meeting Emma every week for the next while.

When she came the next week, with only her mum this time, Clare explained that they would all meet together first and then she would see Emma on her own, if that was okay. Emma's mum seemed to think that it was okay, so Emma went along with it, though she was quite anxious. At that session they did some work on thoughts, feelings and actions. They used drawing and a workbook, which Emma liked, as she did not have to keep answering questions. She was given 'homework' to do, which was really a bit more of what they had been doing in the session. Emma looked forward to the next session, as Clare said they were going to be doing relaxation exercises the next week.

By about the fifth session, Emma thought she was getting the hang of things. She was starting to 'boss back' her worries a bit. She was managing to keep her questions about her worries until her 'worry time' in the evenings, and her mum seemed in better form with her. She had asked one of the girls in her class to play skipping with her at break and was starting to look forward to break time instead of dreading it. She was not sure if the relaxation exercises helped, but she liked doing them. She thought her mum and dad were different with her. They were calmer and did not keep asking her if she was okay. She felt a bit more grown up.

After the tenth session, Clare asked Emma and her mum if it would be okay to have the sessions every two weeks from now on. This suited them fine, and after two more sessions, Clare suggested stretching it out to once a month for two more sessions.

Emma has now finished her therapy. She will see Clare again in six months for a 'booster' session, but she and her parents feel they can manage on their own. It won't be straightforward, but Emma has learned many self-help tips for managing her worries, and she will continue to use these. Her parents are confident that they will be able to help her and know they can seek further help if it is needed.

THE ROLE OF MEDICATION

Guidelines for mental health professionals recommend a psychological therapy approach as 'first-line' treatment for anxiety in young people, with medication being considered only for very severe cases or in situations where psychological therapy has not worked. While there are many medications that have powerful anxiety-reducing effects, their role in the treatment of anxiety in young people is complicated. There are a number of reasons for this. First, such medication does reduce anxiety but when it is stopped the anxiety may return, leading to the young person feeling the need to restart medication, which can lead to long-term medication dependence. Also, the reduction in anxiety brought about by medication may mean the young person is less likely to learn coping strategies for dealing with anxiety, which they will need when the medication is stopped. This does not mean that medication has no role. It can be invaluable in the short term in situations of overwhelming anxiety or sleeplessness and has been shown to be of benefit in the treatment of severe depression, which often also involves severe anxiety, and in the treatment of OCD. In both these disorders, medication often helps young people to feel well enough to engage in therapy and to try some of the self-help techniques, and it has been shown that outcomes are best when medication is combined with CBT. Sertraline is the medication most commonly used to treat anxiety in young people. It is an SSRI, which means it blocks the reuptake of serotonin into the nerve cells in the brain, which leads to increased concentrations of serotonin in the spaces between the cells. This may be how SSRI medications lead to a reduction in anxiety, although there may also be other mechanisms for how they work that we do not yet fully understand.

If medication is recommended by the GP or psychiatrist, it is important that full discussion takes place about what it is for, how it should be taken and for how long, how long before the effects will be felt and potential side effects. There is evidence that some of the medications used to treat anxiety disorders may be associated with the young person developing thoughts of suicide or self-harm. This adverse effect is very rare, but discussion should take place with the doctor and the young person about how to manage it, should it occur.

Young people are often reluctant to take medication recommended by their doctor. They may feel that they should be able to manage on their own without the help of medication. They may be afraid of how the medication will affect them. They are often aware of the stigma that still exists about using medication of this kind. They may worry that they will become dependent on medication. Their parents or carers often have the same concerns. These issues should be discussed with the prescribing doctor. There is a very informative website at www.headmeds.org.uk for young people who have had medication recommended for a mental health problem. It is part of the support information provided by Young Minds (www.youngminds.org.uk). In addition to providing all the information needed to make an informed decision, it includes vignettes of young people telling their stories about their experiences of using medication.

Medication should never be the only treatment a young person receives; it should always be accompanied by some form of therapy, and by support for parents and carers. No parent likes to think that their young person needs medication for a mental health problem, but if it is recommended by the doctor for severe or intractable disorders, it is well worth seriously considering its use. I always tell young people who need medication in addition to therapy that medication does not heal them, but it helps them to do the work needed to heal themselves.

CHAPTER **8**

SPECIAL PROBLEMS

This chapter deals with particular problems that parents and carers of young people with anxiety may face. These include nightmares and night terrors, problems with friends, refusal to go for help, school refusal, family difficulties and using alcohol or drugs as a crutch.

NIGHTMARES

We do not know what causes nightmares but, as with adults, nightmares happen more often in young people when they are anxious. They are very common, especially in young children, and involve frightening dreams that generally occur in the second half of the night. Typically the person wakes up alert and distressed and can usually recall the content of the nightmare vividly. They can often recall fragments of the nightmare during the day, and this may make them fearful of going to bed at night.

Providing comfort and reassurance that this is a dream and is not real usually enables the young person to go back to sleep. It is probably not possible to prevent nightmares, but parents are usually advised to have a 'quiet hour' before bedtime and to avoid scary movies and frightening TV programmes during the day. If the young person wants to talk about the nightmare during the day, it is important to provide comfort and a listening ear, but it is best to avoid becoming over-focused on it. Parental anxiety about nightmares is easily transmitted to the young person and may make nightmares occur more often.

NIGHT TERRORS

Night terrors are indeed terrifying to witness. They are also quite common, and they typically occur during the first half of the night, often happening at the same point after the onset of sleep on each occasion. They are similar to nightmares in some ways but are different from them in many ways. The person sits up abruptly in a terrified state, often crying or screaming, with rapid breathing and heart rate. While they appear to be awake, it is not possible to communicate with them. They may appear to be confused and do not respond to reassurance. They may run or jump around, as if trying to flee from something terrible. The episode rarely lasts longer than about 15 minutes, following which they go back to sleep. They usually do not remember anything about it in the morning. It is not known what causes night terrors, but anxiety or illness can make them more likely to occur in people who are prone to them.

People having a night terror rarely injure themselves, and it is best not to try to hold or restrain them, as this often increases their thrashing about and makes them more frightened. It is best to stay in the room, speaking in a soft and calm tone and taking simple safety steps, such as closing doors and windows and ensuring they cannot fall down the stairs. The night terror always passes and the young person has no memory of it the next day. The temptation to question them about it or to go over the event in graphic detail should be avoided, as this may worry them. Despite how they appear during a night terror, there is no evidence that people who have them are more likely to be emotionally disturbed than those who do not have night terrors.

PROBLEMS WITH FRIENDS

Young people with anxiety problems often have problems with friendships. They may be very shy, rarely leaving the house except for obligatory activities such as school attendance, or they may be more sociable, but be unable to handle the ups and downs and ins and outs of childhood and adolescent group dynamics. Chapter 4 has information about helping children with friendships and bullying but much of what hurts anxious young people most is not actual bullying. Many parents will be familiar with the heartbreak experienced by their child when their best friend 'dumps' them and takes up with another best friend or when their teenager is not invited to participate in a longed-for group activity. Your instinct as a parent or teacher is to feel angry with the 'dumpers' or 'excluders', but this does not help. Being able to listen if the young person can talk about how they are feeling is important, as is not giving advice or criticism, even though you may have a good inkling, from your knowledge of the young person, as to what has led to the hurtful situation. Some of the ideas in the previous chapters about identifying and practising social skills may be valuable for younger children but less useful with teenagers. Being able to listen, being a 'secure base', noticing and supporting any tiny fragment of socially appropriate behaviour, encouraging the young person to develop any interest or skill they have and being able to keep in mind that many of the most socially anxious and awkward young people become socially competent and comfortable adults are all valuable skills.

'HE WON'T GO FOR HELP'

This is not uncommon in teenagers who need professional help with anxiety. They may deny there is a problem, despite it being obvious to those who know them that they need help. They may blankly refuse to discuss the situation or simply refuse to go for help. Fear and embarrassment are usually the driving forces behind their refusal, along with a belief that they should be able to sort things out themselves.

With younger children, the problem is easier to manage, as most children in this age group are unable to resist when parents are determined to get them the help they need and to be part of that process with them. Adolescents are frequently unwilling or unable to talk to their parents about their problems for many reasons, including the healthy adolescent drive towards independence. Mentioning that online support is available at www.reachout.com or www.helpguide.org is likely to be rebuffed, but the young person may gain some support from using such resources later in private.

Rather than talk to a parent, the young person may be prepared to talk to a trusted adult who is less emotionally involved, such as a relative or a teacher, who may be able to motivate them to agree to professional help. Sometimes the young person will agree to attend the GP for a check-up, while refusing to attend a counselling or mental health service, and some GPs are able to provide the support needed. In serious situations, such as with young people whose health is being affected by their anxiety problems but who refuse to attend for help, it may be necessary for their parent or guardian to seek advice from their local CAMHS.

Such services are familiar with the difficulty of getting young people to attend. Some will have outreach mental health workers who may be able to link up with the young person and dispel some of their fears about attending.

Involuntary admission to a psychiatric unit is only considered where there is a strong risk that, because of a mental illness, the young person may cause immediate and serious harm to themselves or another person. This is very rarely the case in young people with pure anxiety disorders, but occasionally it may be necessary if a young person is highly suicidal or psychotic. The process for such involuntary admission is governed by legislation, which differs from country to country, but the starting point is the GP in most instances. It is a highly stressful and horrific process for the young person to have to go through, and also for their parent or guardian, but it may be necessary to preserve the young person's life.

SCHOOL REFUSAL

It can take some time to recognize that a young person has school refusal, because it often starts after a period of missing school because of illness of some kind, when it may appear that the young person is not well enough to attend. It may take a month or two before it becomes apparent that the problem is deeper than that. Typically, the young person becomes overwhelmed with anxiety when attempting to go to school or, in some cases, when there is any mention of school. They often function perfectly normally when school is out of the picture and are able and willing to continue school work when at home.

School refusal is usually due to an extreme form of separation anxiety, but occasionally the young person is fearful of something that takes place at school or may take place, such as bullying or exclusion. The longer the young person is out of school, the more difficult it becomes for them to return, as they will be 'out of sync' with both school work and peer relationships in school, and they may have grown to enjoy being at home all day. Very close cooperation between parents and the school is needed to help successfully with school refusal.

SOPHIA'S STORY

Sophia, aged 13, had been out of school for six months. She had moved from primary to secondary school in September and had attended her new school without difficulty for three weeks, but then she got a flu-like illness and was at home for a week.

She said she wanted to go back to school, but whenever this was attempted, she developed nausea and a headache, so it was postponed. When she had been out of school for a month, she saw a paediatrician for a check-up, on the advice of their family doctor. All the tests were normal, and Sophia and her parents were baffled and angry that 'something' had not shown up in the tests, as they had observed how unwell Sophia looked when any attempt was made to get her to attend school. The school understood that she was unwell and were sending work home, which Sophia was completing without difficulty and emailing to her teachers for correction.

Sophia had a good relationship with her parents, who tried many times to talk to her about how she was feeling. She insisted there was nothing wrong with the school; it was just her sick feeling that made it impossible for her to attend. Neither of her parents were forceful by nature, but they tried a number of approaches, including insisting that she got up at the normal school time, dressed in her uniform and went in the car on the school run with her sister, which she complied with, but she always refused to get out of the car and became panic stricken if they tried to force the issue. Some relatives had advised that Sophia should be physically lifted from the car into school, insisting that she would be fine when she was in school, but her parents knew they could not do that.

Sophia's year head suggested that her parents might consider referral to the local CAMHS. Her parents were taken aback, as they had become somewhat resigned to the situation and were considering applying for home tuition for Sophia. The year head pointed out that Sophia's social development was as important as her academic development, and that home tuition could not address that aspect of her education.

Reluctantly, her parents agreed to attend the local CAMHS and, after some persuasion, so did Sophia.

It took a further two months, but gradually Sophia got back to school. She got great support and advice from the psychologist in the CAMHS, who she saw weekly. She learned how to practise relaxation and control her breathing as she worked through a plan of gradual reintroduction to school. This involved initially spending a few minutes in the school entrance hall and gradually spending more time and moving closer to the classroom each day over a three-week period. The school was both supportive and accommodating, having seen this approach work with other pupils with school refusal. Sophia practised how she would answer questions about where she had been and decided to say she had been 'sick' without going into too much detail.

While Sophia attended the psychologist, her parents had sessions with the mental health social worker, who helped them to be clear with Sophia that they expected her to return to school and to encourage and support the progress she was making.

There was a family session, where Sophia's sister and brother were able to express their frustration and anger at what they saw as Sophia's 'special treatment', how much they worried about her and their support for her attempts to get back to school.

Sophia is now 15 and rarely misses a day of school. There is sometimes conflict when she does not come in on time at night and does not say where she is going, but secretly her parents are reassured by this 'normal' teenage behaviour that shows them that she is striving towards independence.

FAMILY DIFFICULTIES

Family relationships impact on the young person with anxiety, and the young person with anxiety impacts on family relationships. Situations that families commonly face include parental disagreement about how best to help the anxious young person, siblings who are hurt and angry about the special treatment they receive, and coping with unhelpful advice from extended family. In turn, the stress generated by these family relationship difficulties tends to make the young person's anxiety worse.

While the vast majority of parents have their child's best interests at heart, they often have differing views about what is in the child's best interests. It is not unusual for one parent to feel that the behaviour of the other parent is contributing to the young person's anxiety. Trying to communicate with each other about these difficult issues is important, as well as remembering to 'press the pause button' and trying to really listen to the other parent's view. If the level of stress is so high that it is impossible to communicate with each other in a helpful way, some joint counselling sessions may be helpful. Even if one parent refuses to attend for joint counselling, the other may be helped by individual counselling.

Siblings may be hurt and angry, often with reason, as young people with anxiety problems can, and sometimes need to, be treated differently. Siblings need to be given some information about why this is happening. This may seem self-evident, but sometimes 'the elephant in the room' is not mentioned by parents out of loyalty to the anxious young person and for fear of making a bad situation worse. A simple explanation may be sufficient, such as, 'Your sister is going through a tough time at the moment, and it is hard for her and for all of us. We are trying to help her, and we are very hopeful that she will sort out her problems soon, but in the meantime we need to make special allowances for her.' Trying to make special time for each of the siblings also helps, and keeping family routines going as far as possible is important, as is taking advantage of any support that is available. If the anxious young person is unable or unwilling to participate in a family outing, maybe they could stay with a responsible relative while the rest of the family go?

People who give unwanted advice can be extremely annoying. They rarely understand the full picture and their advice is often hurtful, but it can be useful to remind yourself that they are usually only trying to be helpful. It may be useful to tell someone who is giving you unsolicited advice that you would like to have a break from talking or thinking about your anxious young person, as that would be most helpful for you.

USING ALCOHOL OR DRUGS AS A CRUTCH

In Western cultures, alcohol is widely used as a crutch to ease social relationships. Many young people drink large amounts before going out to clubs or discos, where they then drink more. Young people with anxiety problems may 'self-medicate' with alcohol, making them particularly susceptible to this pattern of drinking and may find they need to have alcohol before any social encounter, leading to dependence.

It can be difficult to recognize when alcohol use has crossed the line from being a useful 'social lubricant' to becoming a dangerous and damaging way of coping. Most people would agree that if the young person's drinking is leading to social, relationship, health or family problems, the line has been crossed and some sort of intervention is needed. Sensible advice, such as cutting down the amount of money available to the young person and limiting the amount and use of alcohol in the home, makes sense, but in reality this will not deter a young person who is dependent on alcohol.

Getting help for the young person is easier said than done. Denial goes hand in hand with excessive alcohol use, and parents are often wary of making an issue of it, for fear of making things worse. If you are concerned about a young person's excessive drinking, it can help to find out what services are available locally for young people with alcohol-related problems and to seek their advice in how to engage the young person. You will need to talk to the young person about your concerns, but having this information in advance is useful.

Young people with anxiety problems may use drugs in a similar way to alcohol, and the same dilemmas may arise. Many adolescents use cannabis in a way that does not seem to be harmful, but some research suggests that regular cannabis use in early adolescence may increase the risk for developing schizophrenia in adult life (Arsenault *et al.* 2002). It can be hard to recognize when cannabis use is leading to psychological dependence, but if parents are concerned, it is worth discussing with a professional how best to proceed in trying to get the young person to seek help.

Dealing with these problems is extremely stressful for parents and carers, and in order to be able to help your young person, you need to be as well as you can be yourself. Some of the ideas on managing your own anxiety in Chapter 3 might be useful.

CHAPTER **9**

WHAT DOES THE FUTURE HOLD?

Parents and carers often worry about how young people with anxiety disorders will cope with adult life. This chapter reviews the studies that have followed anxious children into adult life. It highlights the risk and protective factors associated with adult outcomes and gives guidance on how protective factors can be fostered.

How do young people with anxiety problems cope with adult life? How do they manage when they no longer have the day-to-day support of their parents, carers or teachers? Will they continue to have symptoms of anxiety? How will they function at work? Will they be able to sustain healthy relationships? Will they become dependent on medication or street drugs? Will they develop depression or other mental health problems? These are all common concerns of parents and carers.

A number of research studies have followed up young people diagnosed with anxiety disorders in childhood to see how they manage as adults (Beesdo, Knappe and Pine 2009; Wittchen *et al.* 2000; Woodward and Fergusson 2001). To put these studies into context, it is important to keep in mind that the young people studied all had a diagnosable anxiety disorder in their childhood. Their diagnosis was based on assessment when they attended clinical services or when they were screened as part of a large population study. There are many young people who suffer from anxiety but who do not fit the criteria for a diagnosable anxiety disorder, because their symptoms are not severe enough, they do not have a sufficient number of symptoms or they are able to function despite their symptoms. The results of the research studies mentioned above may not be the same for these young people as for those with a diagnosable anxiety disorder. Also, few studies have followed up with adults beyond the age of 30, as long-term studies of this type are very expensive and hard to do.

Despite differences in how these studies were carried out, and in the length of follow-up, they all tend to show similar results. About 80 per cent of young people who have a diagnosable anxiety disorder in adolescence no longer have an anxiety disorder when reassessed two, three or four years later. Those with the most severe disorders at baseline, and those with the greatest number of disorders, are most likely to be in the 20 per cent who still have an anxiety disorder at follow-up. When longer follow-up studies are done, the results show that having a diagnosable anxiety disorder in adolescence increases the risk of developing anxiety and depression in adult life. The risk of developing a substance abuse disorder (excessive use of alcohol or drugs) is also increased. What all this means is that anxiety disorders tend to wax and wane throughout life and that the chances of 'getting over' a childhood anxiety disorder are very high, but there is some risk of being further troubled by anxiety, depression or excessive use of alcohol or drugs in adult life. Evidence is not available to be clear about how high this risk is, but studies have shown that many people who were troubled with anxiety in childhood are no longer troubled in adult life, and there is reason to be optimistic.

WHAT DOES THE FUTURE HOLD FOR MY CHILD?

Every parent and carer would like to know if there is any way of predicting the outcome for their particular young person. Unfortunately, there is not. The research studies that have been done involve statistics that tell us what factors are associated with risk and resilience in the study group, but they cannot tell us how these relate to any individual young person. This is because mental health disorders are caused by a very complex interplay between biological factors (such as genetic traits), psychological factors (such as the child's personality style, confidence level and ability to problem-solve), and social factors (such as socio-economic group, parenting style, school environment and peer group experiences). Research can identify many of these factors but cannot tell us how they interact with one another in any particular young person.

IS THERE EVIDENCE TO POINT US IN THE RIGHT DIRECTION?

There is good evidence that parental warmth, nurturance and acceptance are associated with less anxiety in young people. This is a consistent finding, whether based on studies that directly observe interactions between parents and their children or whether the studies are based on self-reports of parents and children (Scott, Scott and McCabe 1991; Wood *et al.* 2003; Siqueland, Kendall and Steinberg 1996). Even this evidence is not clear-cut, as it is mostly based on studies carried out on a one-off basis at a particular point in time, which shows an association but not the direction of the association. Thus, for example, most studies show that a warm style of parenting that encourages autonomy is associated with less anxiety in the child, and while a more controlling style of parenting is associated with more anxiety, it is not clear which came first. It may be that children with low anxiety levels promote a parenting style that is warm and non-controlling, or it may be that a controlling parenting style fosters anxiety in the child. We know that anxiety is 'contagious', and it is likely that adult anxiety and child anxiety feed off each other, such that it does not really matter which came first. The research suggests that it is beneficial for children if the adults involved in their lives manage their own anxiety and encourage independence and autonomy in their children. Taking active steps to look after your own physical and mental health provides a good role model for your young person, while encouraging them to use strategies for managing their anxiety (see Chapter 3) gives them effective tools that they can use throughout their lives.

FIONA'S STORY

Fiona is 42 and has two children – Mia aged ten and Mike aged five. She can 'see herself' in Mia, who is a sensitive, shy child who becomes easily upset if there is any change in her routine and who worries a lot. Fiona remembers her own teenage years, when she had to 'see someone' for help with anxiety. She can remember how bewildered and confused she felt, and she very much wants things to be different for Mia. As an adult, Fiona has often felt anxious or worried, but she has never been overcome by symptoms of anxiety as she was when younger.

She has tried to pinpoint what helped her to get through those difficult years and what helps her now. She can remember a little about the counsellor she saw as a teenager, who seemed to view her as entirely normal at a time when Fiona thought of herself as 'crazy'. She can remember the relief of being accepted as she was, of not being told what to do, and of some of the things that the counsellor said might help, like 'worry time' and relaxation exercises, which she sometimes uses still. She can remember vividly how supportive her mother was in bringing her to appointments and how patient she was while encouraging her to try new things. She often wonders what her dad made of the whole situation. He never spoke to her about her problems, but would often ask her if she was okay, and he was very tolerant of her moodiness. She thinks that a teacher in her school, who seemed to understand how she was feeling, also played a big part in helping her. This teacher seemed to see beyond the anxious and quiet teenager and always had high expectations of Fiona. She often thinks that what she went through as a teenager has made her much more empathic and tolerant of other people, who she rarely judges, as she realizes that you never really know what is going on in other people's lives.

Fiona has learned over the years how important it is for her to look after herself. She has a good relationship with her partner Todd, who is Mike's but not Mia's father. She enjoys healthy eating and cooking, so that is not a problem. She runs once a week with a friend and enjoys the feeling of well-being this brings. She notices her anxiety levels rising when work is particularly stressful or when there is a row at home but has learned how it helps to talk things through and not to bottle things up. She tries to encourage Mia to talk about how she is feeling, but she does not push her, as she knows this does not help. Mia has a few friends and seems happy in school, which reassures Fiona.

Fiona sometimes worries about what the teenage years will be like for both Mia and Mike, but she does not dwell on these thoughts, as she knows that no one can foretell the future. She does not talk much about her anxiety but when she does she often says, 'Most people have something they are coping with – mine is anxiety.' She feels she understands herself reasonably well and has built in to her life many things that help her manage her anxiety. She regards herself as an optimistic person, and she looks forward to the future, which she hopes will be bright for her family and for herself.

The future is likely to bring major advances in the pharmaceutical industry, with the development of 'tailored' drugs for the treatment of anxiety, which will interact with the individual's specific genetic profile in ways that improve efficacy and reduce side effects. Marketing techniques will also improve, potentially leading to increased usage of such medication. This is likely to be balanced by those who hold a more holistic view, who advocate the importance of relationships, healthy diet, exercise, drinking in moderation, social connectedness and attending to spiritual needs in managing anxiety, which they regard as part of life. It is hoped that these differing viewpoints can complement each other, taking on board the importance of the holistic approach, while appreciating the valuable role that medication can play in the treatment of the most severe forms of anxiety.

Research has repeatedly shown the key role that supportive relationships with family and school play in both preventing and managing anxiety and other mental health problems in young people (Resnick *et al.* 1997; Ginsburg *et al.* 2014). As a parent, teacher or carer, your support, encouragement and hope for the future are your young person's most important assets. The road you walk with them may be long and hard, but your support will make a great difference. And remember, in order to look after others well, you need to look after yourself. Good luck with your invaluable job!

RESOURCES

RESOURCES IN YOUR COMMUNITY

- Family and friends
- Your child's school counsellor
- Your GP, who may be able to help directly, or may advise on local counselling or mental health services for young people
- Your local CAMHS – referral is usually made by the GP
- The young person's social worker, if they have one
- In a crisis, the local hospital accident and emergency department

USEFUL BOOKS

Cresswell, C. and Willetts, L. (2007) *Overcoming Your Child's Fears and Worries: A Self-Help Guide Using Cognitive Behavioral Techniques.* London: Robinson Publishing.

Written mainly for parents, this book is easy to read and has good advice. It focuses on a cognitive behavioural therapy approach, which is often very helpful.

Chansky, T. E. (2004) *Freeing Your Child From Anxiety.* New York, NY: Broadway Books.

Rapee, R., Wignall, A., Spence, S. and Lyneham, H. (2008) *Helping Your Anxious Child: A Step-by-Step Guide for Parents.* Oakland, CA: New Harbinger Publications.

Both of the above books, which focus on a cognitive behavioural therapy approach, are useful for parents, particularly those living in the USA.

Dacey, J. S,. and Fiore, L. B. (2002) *Your Anxious Child: How Parents and Teachers can Relieve Anxiety in Children.* San Francisco, CA: Jossey-Bass.

Foxman, P. (2004) *The Worried Child: Recognizing anxiety in Children and Helping Them Heal.* Alameda, CA: Hunter House Inc.

These books published in the USA give a comprehensive overview of the causes of anxiety and approaches to treatment, with information for both parents and teachers.

Lewis, D. (2002) *Helping Your Anxious Child.* London: Vermilion, part of Ebury Publishing.

This book contains many helpful techniques to help children both at home and at school.

USEFUL ORGANIZATIONS

Samaritans: A 24-hour service offering confidential support to anyone who is in a crisis.

Telephone Helpline UK: 0845 790 9090

Telephone Helpline Ireland: 116 123

Telephone Helpline USA: +1 (800) 273 TALK

Telephone Helpline Australia: 13 25 47

Befrienders Worldwide: Contact details for helplines in many countries throughout the world: www.befrienders.org.

YoungMinds: A UK-based charity committed to improving the mental health of all young people. It runs a parents' helpline, which offers free, confidential online and telephone support and advice to any adult with concerns about the mental health of a young person up to the age of 25 years.

Tel: 0808 802 5544
email: parents@youngminds.org.uk
website: www.youngminds.org.uk.

USEFUL WEBSITES

www.anxietybc.com

An excellent Canadian website with practical information and self-help guidance for young people, parents and carers. It includes video clips of young people talking about how they cope with anxiety.

www.childanxiety.net

The Child Anxiety Network's website, which provides user-friendly information for parents, carers and young people.

www.reachout.com

An interactive and informative website for young people, with convincing stories from real young people about how they coped with anxiety and many other difficulties.

www.youngminds.org.uk

The website of a UK-based charity committed to improving the mental health of all young people. It contains good advice for parents and carers about how to help and how to access services in the UK, and a survival guide for parents.

www.headmeds.org.uk

A website run by YoungMinds, with extensive information for young people and their parents and carers about medication used in the treatment of mental health problems.

www.mind.org.uk

The website of a UK mental health charity, with an informative section on anxiety.

www.helpguide.org/topics/anxiety.htm

An American website with international relevance that includes useful information on anxiety for adults and children.

www.kidshealth.org

An American website with extensive information and advice on all aspects of children's health, behaviour and development, using jargon-free language. It includes articles, animation and games for children and teenagers relating to many physical and mental health problems.

www.aboutourkids.org

The New York University Child Study Center's website, which provides information on children's mental health and parenting based on research in child psychiatry, psychology and child development.

www.rcpsych.ac.uk

The website of the Royal College of Psychiatrists in the UK. Click 'health advice', and then 'parents and youth info' for information for parents, carers and young people about a range of issues including anxiety.

www.aacap.org

The American Academy of Child and Adolescent Psychiatry's website. Click 'facts for families'.

www.tourettes-action.org.uk

The website of a support organization in the UK for people with Tourette's disorder, which provides much information for young people, parents and teachers. It includes a moderated forum where people with Tourette's disorder can 'chat' with one another.

www.decd.sa.gov.au

The Government of South Australia's Department for Education and Child Development (DECD) website. Enter 'anxiety' into the search engine on the webpage to access links to excellent information for parents, carers, teachers, and young people.

www.spunout.ie

An informative Irish website dealing with many issues affecting young people. It includes a wide-ranging guide to support services for young people in Ireland.

www.worrywisekids.org

An American website with useful information for parents and carers about all aspects of anxiety in young people.

REFERENCES

American Psychiatric Association (1994) *Diagnostic and Statistical Manual of the Mental Disorders (4th Edition)*, Washington, DC: American Psychiatric Association.

Arntz, A. (2003) 'Cognitive therapy versus applied relaxation as treatment of generalized anxiety disorder.' *Behaviour Research and Therapy 41*, 633–646.

Arsenault, L., Cannon, M., Poulton, R., Murray, R., Caspi, A. and Moffitt, T. E. (2002) 'Cannabis use in adolescence and risk for adult psychosis: Longitudinal prospective study.' *British Medical Journal 325*, 1212–1213.

Barrett, P. M. and Sonderegger, R. (2005) 'Anxiety in Children: FRIENDS Program.' In: A. Freeman (ed.), *Encyclopedia of Cognitive Behaviour Therapy*. New York: Kluwer Academic/Plenum Publishers.

Beesdo, K., Knappe, S. and Pine, D. S. (2009) 'Anxiety and anxiety disorders in children and adolescents. Developmental issues and implications for DSM-V.' *Psychiatric Clinics of North America, 32,* 483–524.

Biederman, J., Newcorn, J. and Sprich, S. (1991) 'Comodity of attention deficit hyperactivity disorder with conduct, depressive, anxiety, and other disorders.' *The American Journal of Psychiatry 148*, 564–577.

Callaghan, M. and The HBSC Ireland Team (2012) *HBSC Ireland Research Factsheet No. 9: Bullying Others among Schoolchildren in Ireland*. Galway: National University of Ireland.

Carek, P. J., Laibstain, S. E. and Carek, S. M. (2011) 'Exercise for the treatment of depression and anxiety.' *International Journal of Psychiatry in Medicine 41*, 15–28.

Chian, L. L., Weinert, C. R., Heiderscheit, A., Tracy, M. F. *et al.* (2013) 'Effect of patient-directed music intervention on anxiety and sedative exposure in critically ill patients receiving mechanical ventilatory support: A randomized clinical trial.' *Journal of the American Medical Association 309*, 2335–2344.

Compton, S. N., March, J. S., Brent, D., Albano, A. M., Weersing, R. and Curry, J. (2004) 'Cognitive-behavioural psychotherapy for anxiety and depressive disorders in children and adolescents: An evidence-based medicine review.' *Journal of the American Academy of Child and Adolescent Psychiatry 43*, 930–959.

Ginsburg, G. S., Becker, E. M., Keeton, C.P., Sakolsky, D *et al.* (2014) 'Naturalistic follow-up of youths treated for pediatric anxiety disorders.' *JAMA Psychiatry 71*, 310–318.

Hawton, K. K. E., Redham, K., Evans, E. and Weatherall, R. (2002) 'Deliberate self-harm in adolescents: Self report survey in schools in England.' *British Medical Journal 325*, 1207–1211.

Kendall, P. C. and Hedtke, K. (2006) *Cognitive-Behavioral Therapy for Anxious Children: Therapist Manual* (3rd edition). Ardmore, PA: Workbook Publishing.

Larun, L., Nordheim, L. V., Ekeland, E., Hagen, K. B. and Heian, F. (2006) 'Exercise in the prevention and treatment of anxiety and depression among children and young people.' *Cochrane Database of Systematic Reviews 3*: CD004691.

Lock, J. and Le Grange, D. (2005) *Helping Your Teenager Beat an Eating Disorder.* New York, NY: The Guilford Press.

Lupien, S. J., McEwen, B. S., Gunnar, M. R., Heim, C. (2009) 'Effects of stress throughout the lifespan on the brain, behaviour and cognition.' *Nature Reviews Neuroscience, 10*, 434–445.

Meltzer, H., Gatward, G., Goodman, R. and Ford, T. (2000) *Mental Health of Children and Adolescents in Great Britain.* London: The Stationery Office.

O'Moore, M. (1997) *Nationwide Study on Bullying Behaviour in Irish Schools.* Dublin: Anti-Bullying Centre, Trinity College Dublin.

Otto, M. W. and Smits, J. A. (2011) *Exercise for Mood and Anxiety: Proven Strategies for Overcoming Depression and Enhancing Well-Being.* New York, NY: Oxford University Press.

Resnick, M. D., Bearman, P. S., Blum, R. W., Bauman, K. E. *et al.* (1997) 'Protecting adolescents from harm: Findings from the national longitudinal study on adolescent health.' *Journal of the American Medical Association 278*, 823–832.

Saphire-Bernstein, S., Way, B. M., Kim, H. S., Sherman, D. K. and Taylor, S. E. (2011) 'Oxytocin receptor gene (OXTR) is related to psychological resources.' *Proceedings of the National Academy of Sciences of the United States of America 108*, 15118–15122.

Scott, W. A., Scott, R. and McCabe, M. (1991) 'Family relationships and children's personality: A cross-cultural and cross-source comparison.' *British Journal of Social Psychology 30*, 1–20.

Shields, M. A. and Wheatley Price, S. (2005) 'Exploring the economic and social determinants of psychological well-being and perceived social support in England.' *Journal of the Royal Statistical Society, Series A 168*, 513–545.

Siqueland, L., Kendall, P. C. and Steinberg, L. (1996) 'Anxiety in children: Perceived family environments and observed family interaction.' *Journal of Clinical Child Psychology 25*, 225–237.

Sullivan, C., Arensman, E., Keeley, H., Corcoran, P. and Perry, I. J. (2004) *Young People's Mental Health: A Report of the Results from the Lifestyle and Coping Survey.* Cork: The National Suicide Research Foundation.

Thirlwall, K., Cooper, P. J., Karalus, J., Voysey, M., Willetts, L. and Cresswell, C. (2013) 'Treatment of child anxiety disorders via guided parent-delivered cognitive-behavioural therapy: Randomised controlled trial.' *British Journal of Psychiatry 203*, 436–444.

Thomas, L. (2002) 'Poststructuralism and therapy – What's it all about?' *International Journal of Narrative Therapy and Community Work 2*, 85–89.

Wittchen, H. U., Lieb, R., Pfister, H. and Schuster, P. (2000) 'The waxing and waning of mental disorders: Evaluating the stability of syndromes of mental disorder in the population.' *Comprehensive Psychiatry 41,* 2, Suppl. 1, 122–132.

Wood, J. J., McLeod, B. D., Sigman, M., Hwang, W. C. and Chu, B. C. (2003) 'Parenting and childhood anxiety: Theory, empirical findings and future directions.' *Journal of Child Psychology and Psychiatry 44*, 134–151.

Woodward, L. J. and Fergusson, D. M. (2001) 'Life course outcomes of young people with anxiety disorders in adolescence.' *Journal of the American Academy of Child and Adolescent Psychiatry 40*, 1086–1093.

INDEX